Vincent's Trees

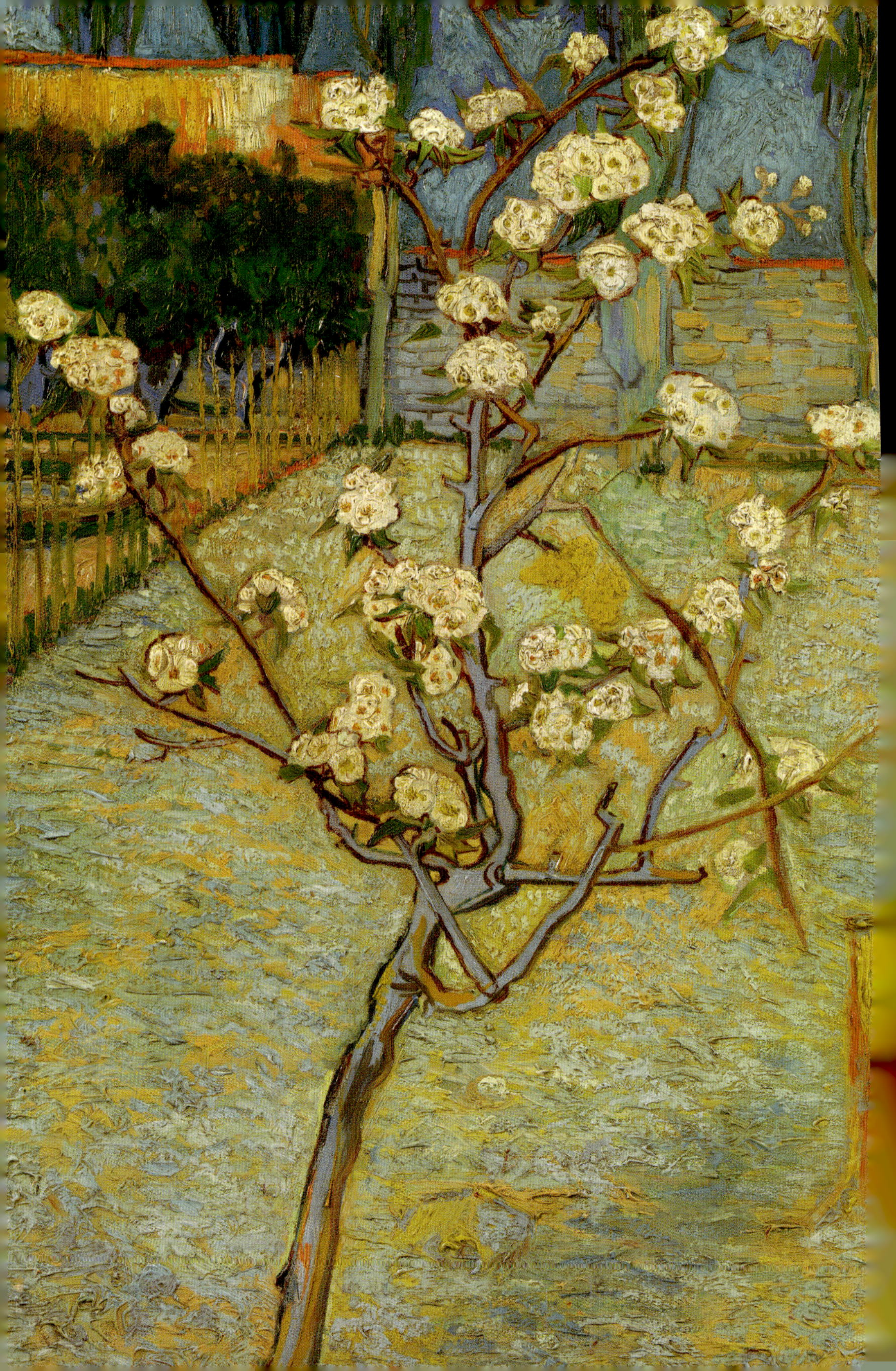

Vincent's Trees

Paintings and Drawings by Van Gogh

Ralph Skea

With 75 illustrations

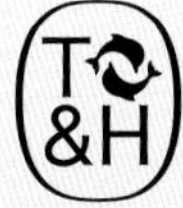

In memory of my mother, Thelma Rathjen Skea

Ralph Skea worked as a town planner and architect, and was for many years
Senior Lecturer in European Urban Conservation at the University of Dundee,
Scotland. He is a painter, and his works have been exhibited widely since 1973.
He is the author of *Vincent's Gardens*.

Quotations are taken from *Vincent van Gogh – The Letters*, published in 2009 by
Thames & Hudson. The number of the letter is in brackets after each excerpt.

Unless otherwise indicated, all works are paintings in oil on canvas.

FRONT COVER
[10] *The Mulberry Tree* (detail), Saint-Rémy, October 1889

BACK COVER AND OPPOSITE
[57] *Branches with Almond Blossom* (detail), Saint-Rémy, February 1890

PAGE 2
[16] *Small Pear Tree in Blossom* (detail), Arles, April 1888

PAGE 12
[12] *Landscape at Twilight* (detail), Auvers-sur-Oise, June 1890

PAGE 52
[46] *Chestnut Trees in Blossom* (detail), Auvers-sur-Oise, May 1890

PAGE 70
[53] *Flowering Orchard*, (detail), Arles, April–May 1888

PAGE 92
[75] *Road with Cypress and Star* (detail), Saint-Rémy, May 1890

First published in the United Kingdom in 2013 by
Thames & Hudson Ltd, 181A High Holborn, London WC1V 7QX

First published in the United States of America in 2013 by
Thames & Hudson Inc., 500 Fifth Avenue, New York, New York 10110

Reprinted 2023

British Library Cataloguing-in-Publication Data
A catalogue record for this book is available from the British Library

Library of Congress Control Number 2012943002
ISBN 978-0-500-23904-9

Printed and bound in China by Everbest Printing Investment Ltd

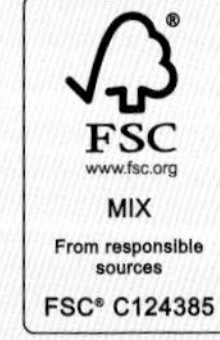

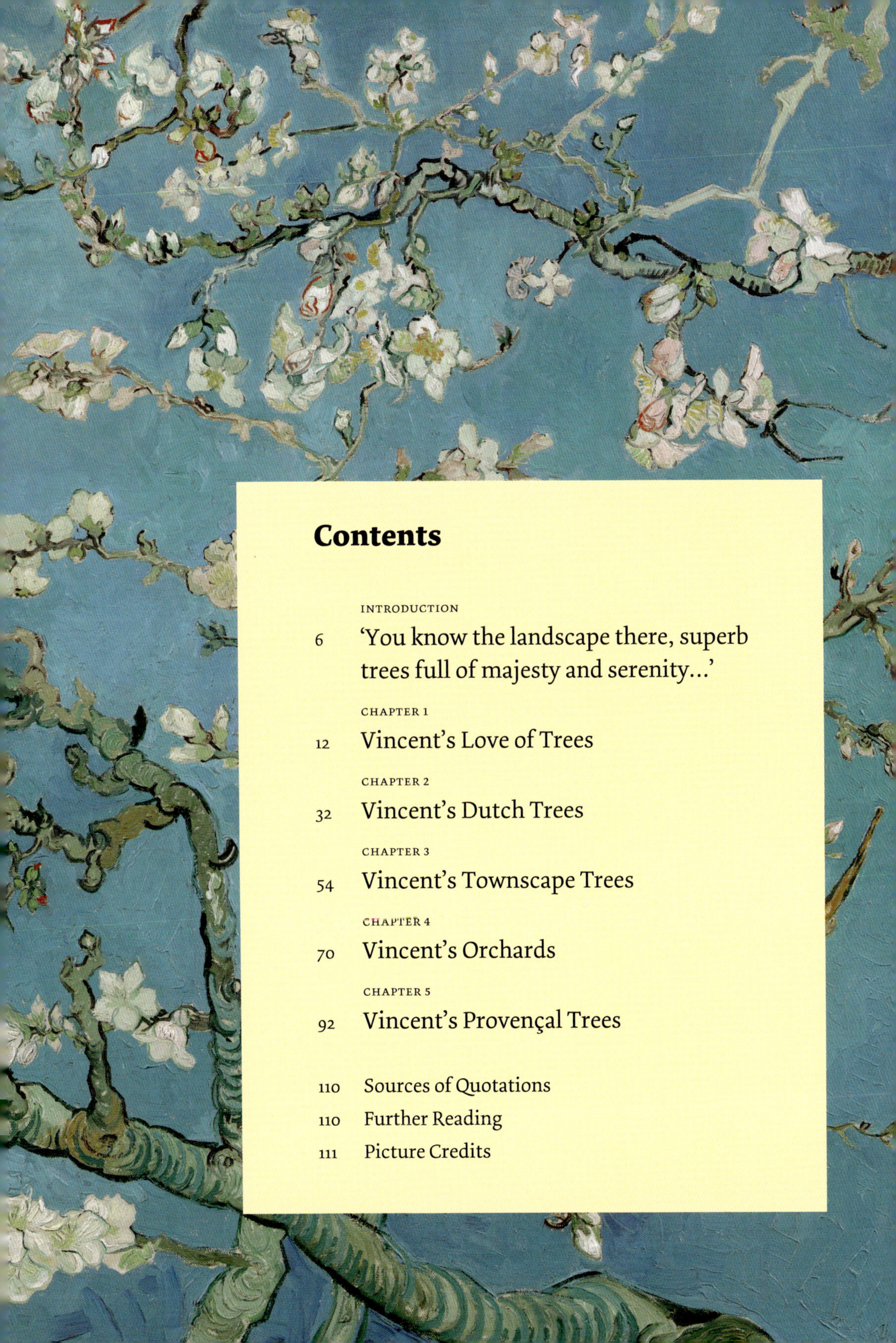

Contents

Introduction:
'You know the landscape there, superb trees full of majesty and serenity...'

A s a painter and draughtsman, Vincent van Gogh (1853–1890) was attracted by tree imagery throughout his exceedingly short career, which lasted from 1880 to 1890. After his belated decision, at the age of twenty-seven, to become a full-time artist, he created memorable drawings and paintings of trees both in rural and urban settings – country roads, woods and orchards, city avenues, town parks and suburban gardens. Many of his most famous works feature both deciduous and evergreen tree species painted in all four seasons.

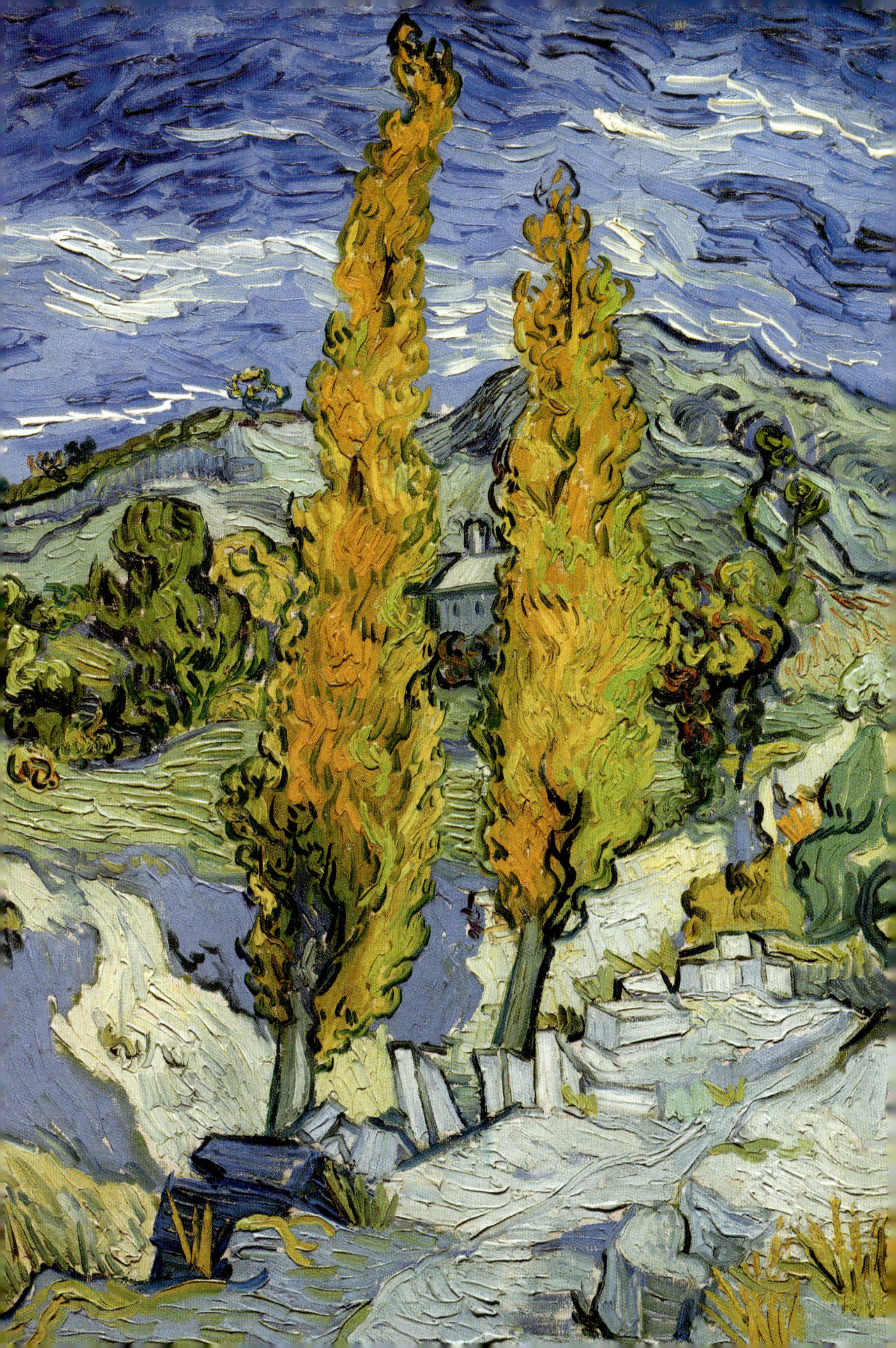

Van Gogh was captivated by the powerful visual presence of trees in the landscape. His drawings and paintings of trees possess highly elaborate, formal qualities determined by the distinctive shapes of tree trunks, traceries of branches and contorted patterns of roots. In the flat countryside of the Netherlands, where he grew up and worked as an artist until November 1885, the verticality of single trees and long, tree-lined avenues created a dramatic impact much greater than that of trees in hilly landscapes. Some of Van Gogh's first drawings depict the typical country lanes of his home province of North Brabant [1]. When Van Gogh started to paint in oil, after teaching himself to draw by using instruction manuals, he explored the rich colours of trees and woods, especially during the autumn months [2].

In many of his tree drawings and paintings, Van Gogh gave the images a deliberate symbolic resonance – blossoming orchards became emblems of rebirth and hope, while the isolated, pollarded tree symbolized the forces of decay and death. These artistic concerns place Van Gogh's tree works firmly within nineteenth-century Romantic thought – indeed, a case could be made for his drawings and paintings of trees being the most Romantic of his whole *oeuvre*.

Due to the survival of 819 of Van Gogh's remarkable letters, we know much about his symbolic and anthropomorphic interests and intentions, and his pantheistic beliefs. Now widely regarded as great works of literature, the letters cover the impressive range of Van Gogh's intellectual interests and emotional preoccupations, including poetry, novels, biography, philosophy, religion, psychology, art history, art theory and practice. As well as providing insights into his opinions and fluctuating moods, they are also full of lyrical descriptions of rural landscapes and patterns of urban life. In fact, Van Gogh had at one time considered a career as a writer, and certainly he was – as his earliest letters reveal – a literary artist before he was a visual artist. Thus, throughout this book a selection of quotes from the letters is used to illustrate his thoughts regarding his representations of trees. Of interest are also the skilful letter sketches that Vincent used to depict paintings

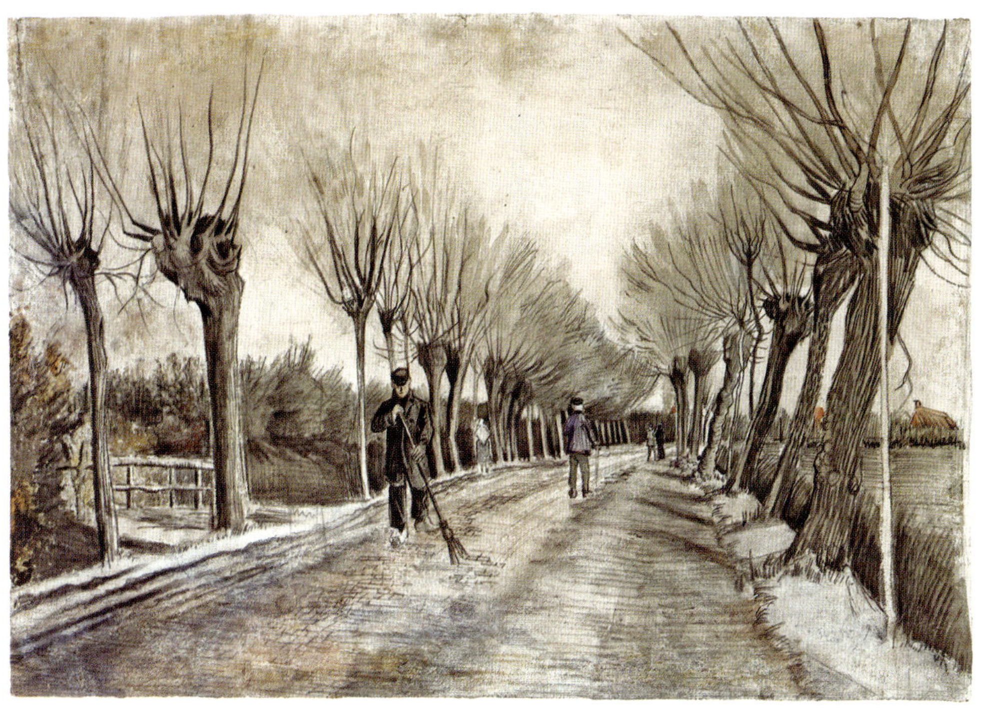

[**1**] *Road in Etten*
Chalk, pencil, pastel and watercolour
on laid paper; pen and brown ink
underdrawing
Etten, October 1881
The pollard willow tree was a
distinctive feature of Vincent's
Dutch homeland. In this very
early drawing, he experimented
with perspective to convey the
dramatic character of the tree-lined
road. He would often 'empathize'
with trees, seeing them as almost
human equivalents. In one letter,
his literary imagination led him
to make explicit anthropomorphic
comparisons between willows and
the aged residents of an almshouse:
'A row of pollard willows sometimes
resembles a procession of orphan
men' (292).

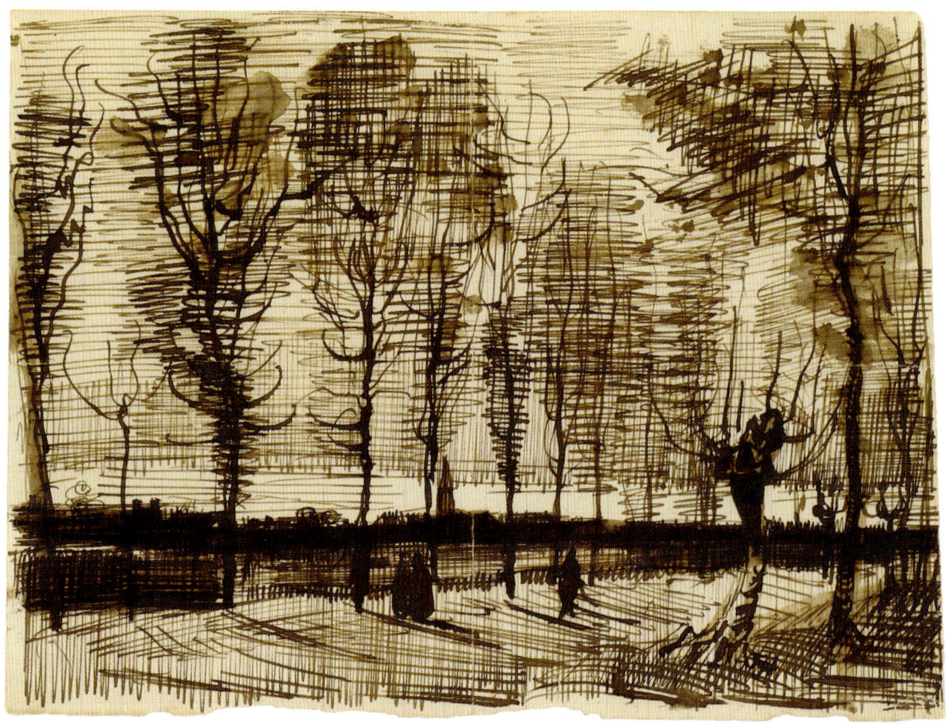

he had just completed or was working on at the time [3]. Overall, the letters provide an invaluable insight into Van Gogh's aesthetic preferences and his intellectual priorities; there was no doubt regarding his epistolary sincerity, as he wrote to his painter friend Anthon van Rappard (1858–1892): 'I'm telling you my thoughts frankly' (176).

Although Vincent van Gogh did not always sign his work, when he decided to do so he always used his first name. And when his brother Theo (1857–1891), who was working as an art dealer in Paris, started to submit his sibling's work for inclusion in prestigious exhibitions, Vincent forbade the use of their family name in catalogues. The reason he most often gave in his letters was that dealers and collectors in France and England would not be able to pronounce his Dutch surname correctly.

Another reason for Van Gogh wishing to become known simply as 'Vincent' was that he had a troubled relationship with many of his relatives: 'In character I'm quite different from the various members of the family, I'm actually *not* a "Van Gogh"' (411). Also, he may have been inspired by the example set by one of his favourite seventeenth-century Dutch artists, Rembrandt Harmenszoon van Rijn (1606–1669), who used his first name to sign all his work.

While the mispronunciation of his family name by non-Dutch speakers remains inevitable, he is known worldwide as Van Gogh despite the signature on his work. Acknowledging Vincent's own preferences, in this book he will be referred to most often simply as 'Vincent'.

The principal reasons for Vincent's fascination with trees are discussed in Chapter 1. His early Dutch period (April 1881 to November 1885), examined in Chapter 2, marked the beginning of his drawings and paintings of trees in gardens, woods and avenues. As Chapter 3 demonstrates, it was not only in the Dutch and French countryside that Vincent found interesting tree species to draw and paint, but also in urban locations – in the villages, towns and cities that he visited or settled in during his ten-year career. In February 1888, he left Paris for the south of France in search of new rural motifs, a warmer climate and brighter colours. Chapters 4 and 5, therefore, explore his response to the distinctive tree species he encountered in rural and urban Provence. Trees, to him, were elements of nature that could become the basis of significant visual art: 'The duty of the painter is to study nature in depth and to use all his intelligence, to put his feelings into his work so that it becomes comprehensible to others' (252).

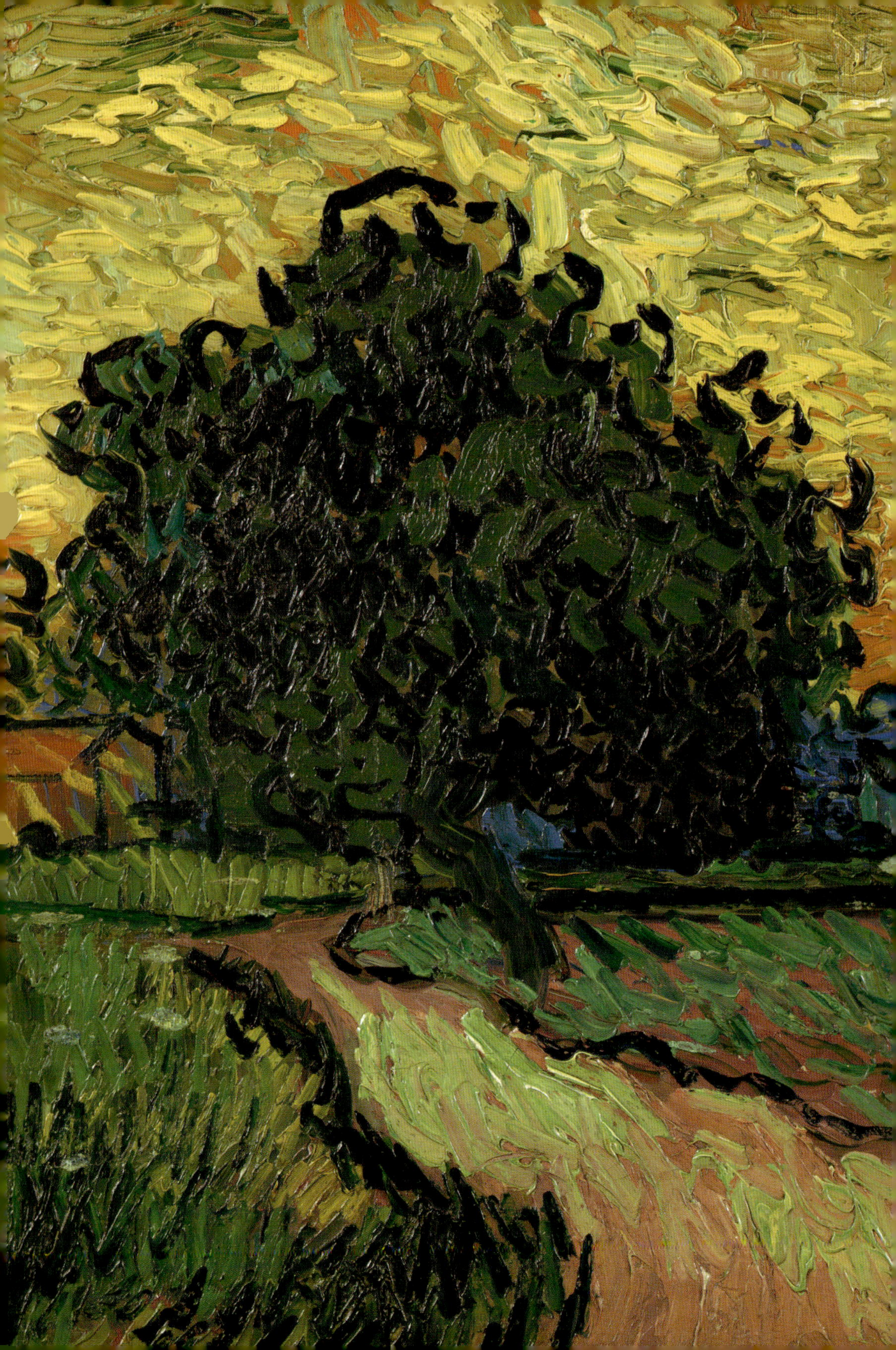

CHAPTER 1

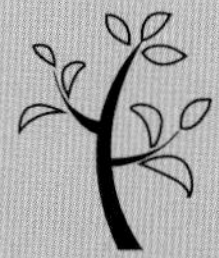

Vincent's Love
of Trees

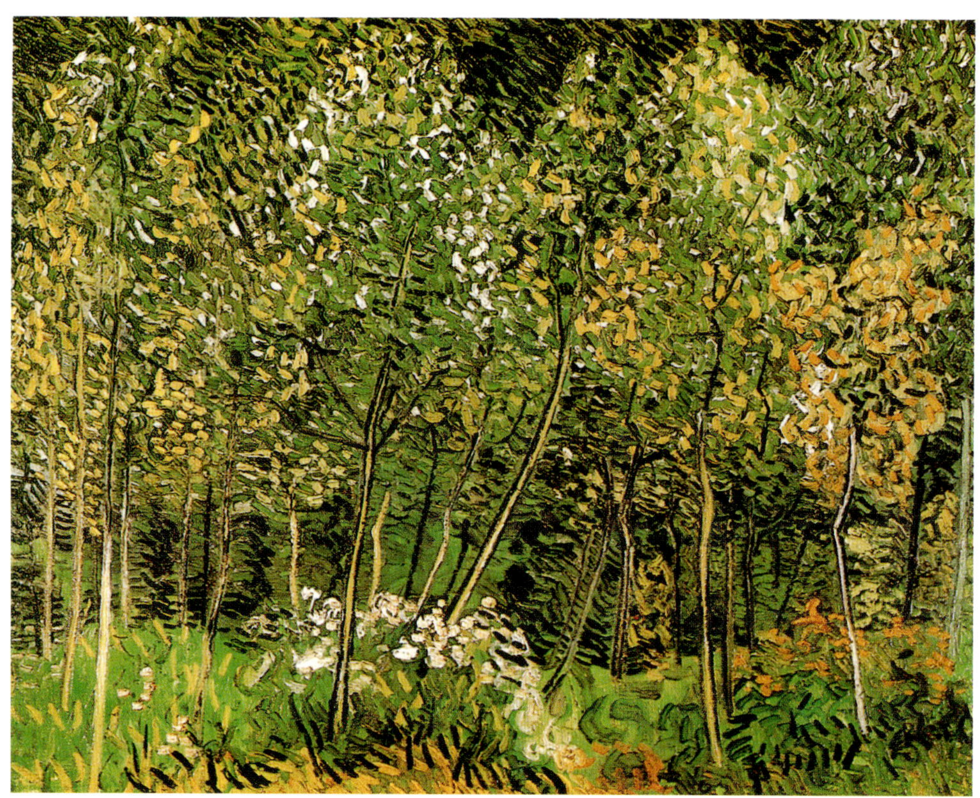

[4] *The Grove*
Auvers-sur-Oise, July 1890
Even in the last few weeks of his
life, Vincent remained enthralled by
the shimmering effects of leaves in
summer woodlands, as this painting
demonstrates. The precise outlining
of the slender tree trunks hints at
Japanese print influences. Overall,
the image has a delicacy that reflects
the character of the saplings.

'And in all of nature, in trees for instance, I see expression and a soul, as it were.'

Nature, for Vincent, possessed a strong emotional significance; he singled out trees as having a particular dynamic force and spiritual essence – an 'expression and a soul' (292). Like many of the nineteenth-century poets he admired – John Keats was an early favourite of his – Vincent idealized nature and viewed the cycle of the seasons as a major subject matter for his art [4]. Even while living in busy towns and cities, he always maintained that his perfect existence would be based in the countryside and spent in close harmony with nature: 'What I think is the best life, oh without even the slightest shadow of doubt, is a life made up of long years of being in touch with nature out of doors' (403). Given his deeply religious outlook, even after he had rejected the Christian church around 1879, he believed that this communion with nature, in all its guises, would somehow lead to contact with the sublime, 'with something on high – unfathomable' (403).

As a consequence, trees were sometimes perceived by him as having quasi-religious qualities, which he felt underpinned all of nature. This pantheistic philosophy of identifying God with nature led Vincent to think that an artist should never draw or paint a tree as if it were just an inert object in the landscape, but always 'empathize' with it as with a fellow creature: 'If one draws a pollard willow as though it were a living being, which it actually is, then the surroundings follow more or less naturally' (175).

Vincent's output as an artist was prodigious, comprising over 900 paintings and 1,100 drawings. Furthermore, all his work was completed in a period of only ten years – one of the shortest careers of any major painter in the history of art. Of course, it is not just the quantity of artworks produced that is so remarkable, but their consistently high quality, from

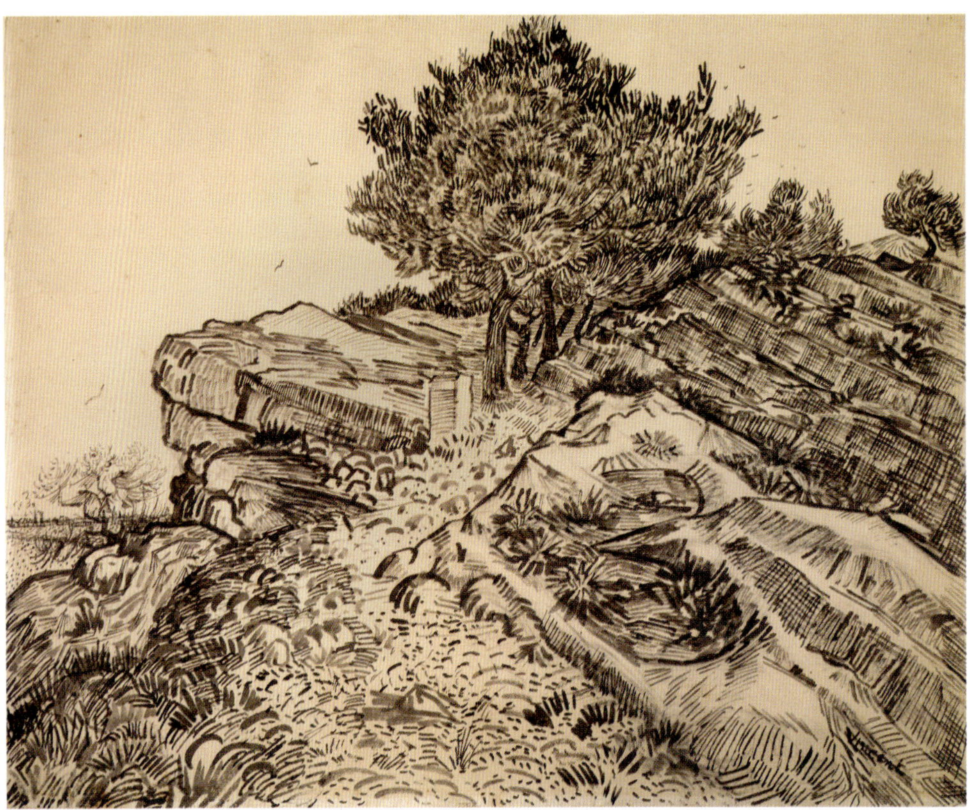

[5] *Rocks and Trees, Montmajour*
Reed pen and ink over graphite on
wove paper
Arles, July 1888
In this late pen drawing, Vincent used a variety of discrete marks to evoke the forms and textures of a wooded hillside. Dots, clusters of lines, and elaborate cross-hatching were employed – almost like a personal shorthand – to convey the visual richness of the terrain with its diagonal rock outcrops.

the hauntingly melancholic compositions of his early Dutch period to the more famous, colourful works produced in the south of France. Regarding his subject matter, Sjaar van Heugten, a leading expert on the artist's work, pointed out that trees played an important role in his landscapes, often constituting their main focus. In fact, about a quarter of his paintings (around 225 canvases) depict groups of trees or a single tree, and a considerable number of Vincent's finest drawings (around 100) make use of tree imagery to explore natural form, texture, symbolism and the anthropomorphic qualities he found in nature [5].

Van Gogh's fascination with trees began early in his life. He was born and raised in the tiny Dutch village of Zundert, in the province of North Brabant, near the border with Belgium. The village was surrounded by heath and extensive pine woods, which Vincent and his siblings enjoyed exploring.

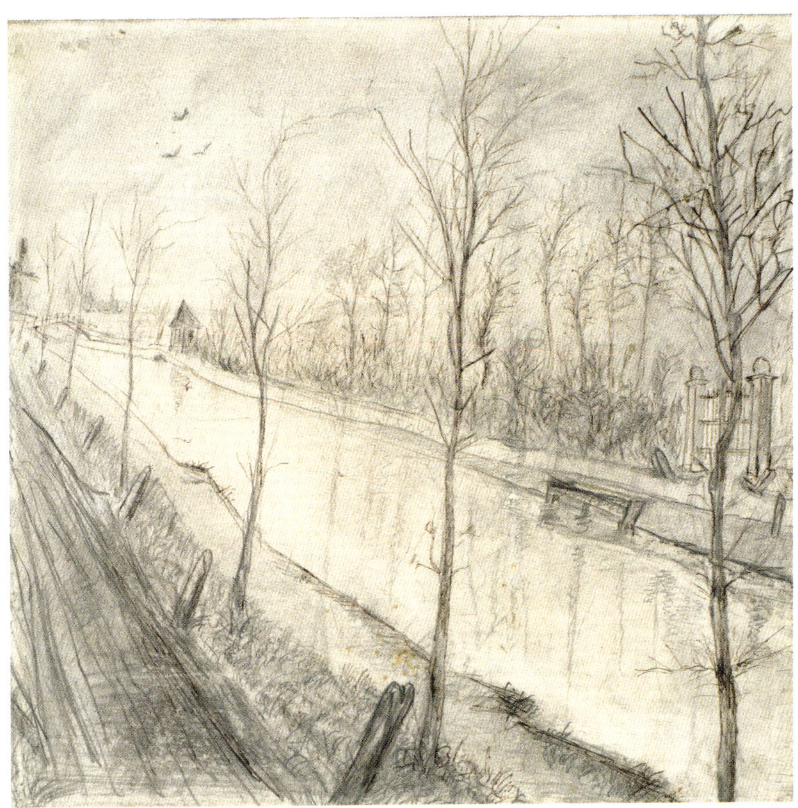

The future artist grew up in a religious environment: his father, Theodorus van Gogh (1822–1885), was a minister of the Groningen branch of the Dutch Reformed Church. More moderate than the strict Calvinist creed of its parent church, the Groningen denomination was influenced by German Romanticism and stressed the importance of absorbing the spiritual forces in nature as a way of achieving communion with God. It is evident that the basic principles espoused by his father's church had a profound influence on Vincent, and laid the foundation for his lifelong reverence for the natural world.

As a young man, Vincent often embarked on long walks, observing nature, and trees in particular, very closely. During his apprenticeship at an art dealer in The Hague in 1873, he completed a number of sensitive drawings of trees growing along canals [6]. Created seven years before he decided to

[6] *Canal*
Pencil and pen in brown ink on wove paper
The Hague, Autumn 1872–Spring 1873
Regularly planted trees along a canal provided the twenty-year-old Vincent with an attractive subject for one of his very first landscape drawings. He took great care in delineating the tree branches and twigs; the image conveys a wistful, slightly melancholic mood.

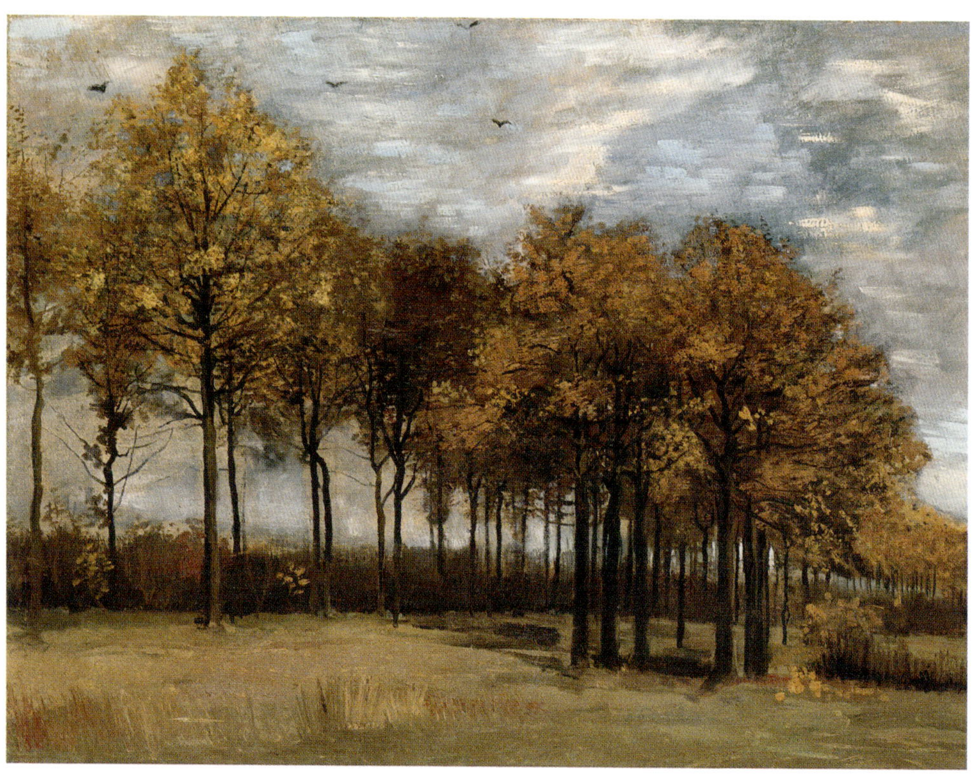

[7] *Autumn Landscape*
Nuenen, October 1885
Vincent marvelled at the visual
richness of the Dutch woodlands
in autumn: 'It's extraordinarily
beautiful here at the moment
with the autumnal effects' (466).
In this work, he juxtaposed a pair
of complementary colours – the
orange-gold of the trees and
groundscape with the blue of the
sky – thus intensifying the visual
effect of the composition.

become an artist, these works demonstrate Vincent's
early interest in the formal impact of trees on the landscape.
Although classified by scholars as the work of a talented
amateur, these images nonetheless possess a distinctive poetic
quality and foreshadow his mature works on the theme.

Later, in 1883, when he was completely committed to his
new calling as an artist, Vincent once again stressed the
importance of long walks in the quest for countryside motifs:
'And then I went out of doors, a long way away, to talk to
nature for a while' (381). As in his boyhood, this conversation
with nature often occurred in woodland settings: quiet,
calm places, full of intriguing shapes, colours and textures,
the woods offered him the opportunity to paint undisturbed,
yet close to towns and cities [7].

While living in North Brabant, Vincent became attracted
by the intricate patterns created by bare tree branches in
the winter months. The elaborate traceries of deciduous

trees lent themselves to his early experiments with the pen
and ink medium [8]. Sometimes, instead of the branches,
it was the complex configuration of tree trunks and roots
that prompted canvases of expressive intensity [9]. But it was
not just woods and groups of trees that caught his attention
as potential subjects for drawings and paintings. Single trees
in the landscape, he believed, could also make for magnificent
motifs, 'If only one has focused all one's attention on that one
tree and hasn't rested until there was some life in it' (175). Parks
and gardens, with their more unusual tree specimens, provided
the artist with secluded spaces where he could explore the
visual harmony produced by overlapping leaf patterns.

[8] *The Kingfisher*
Pencil, pen and brush in brown ink
(originally black), heightened with
opaque white paint, on wove paper
Nuenen, March 1884
This very precise drawing was
inspired by a poem by the French
painter and writer Jules Breton
(1827–1906). Vincent's lyrical
rendering of the patterns of the
tree trunks and bare branches
resulted in a calm image – the
stillness seems to be broken
only by the flight of the bird.

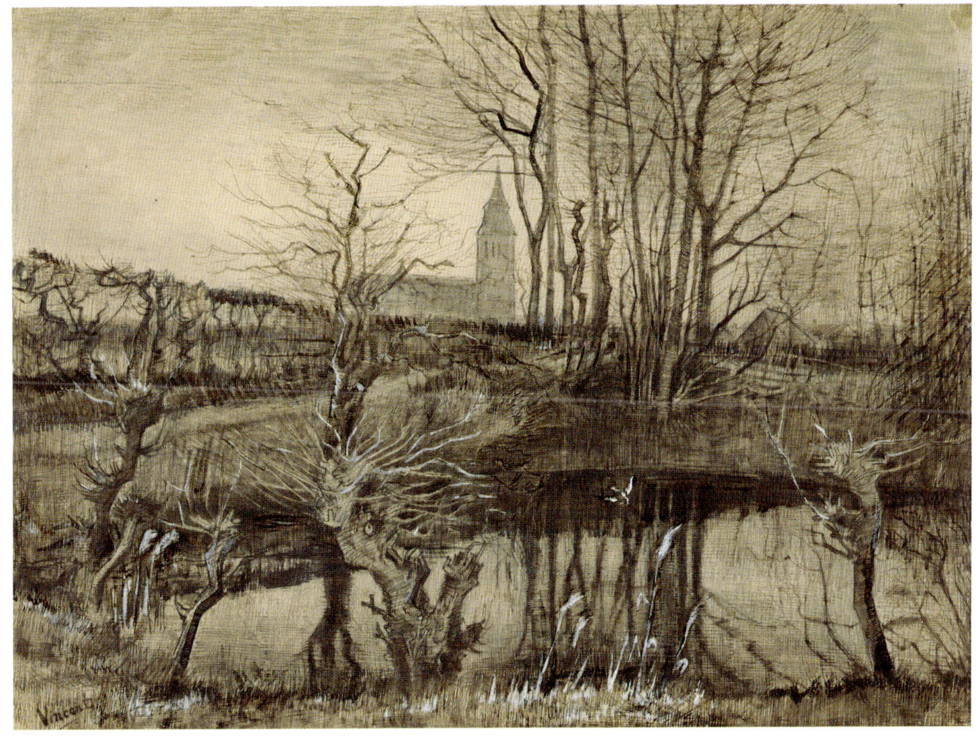

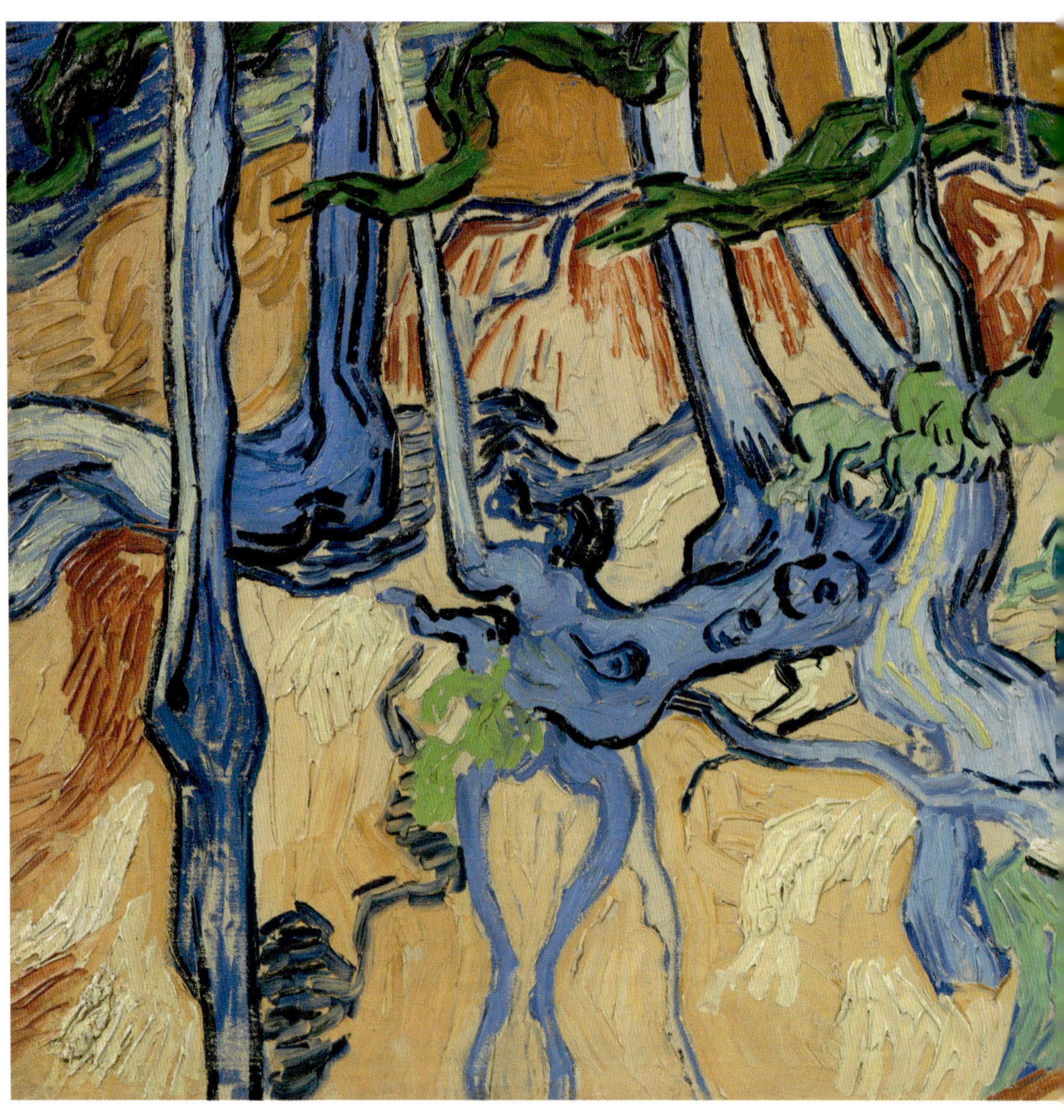

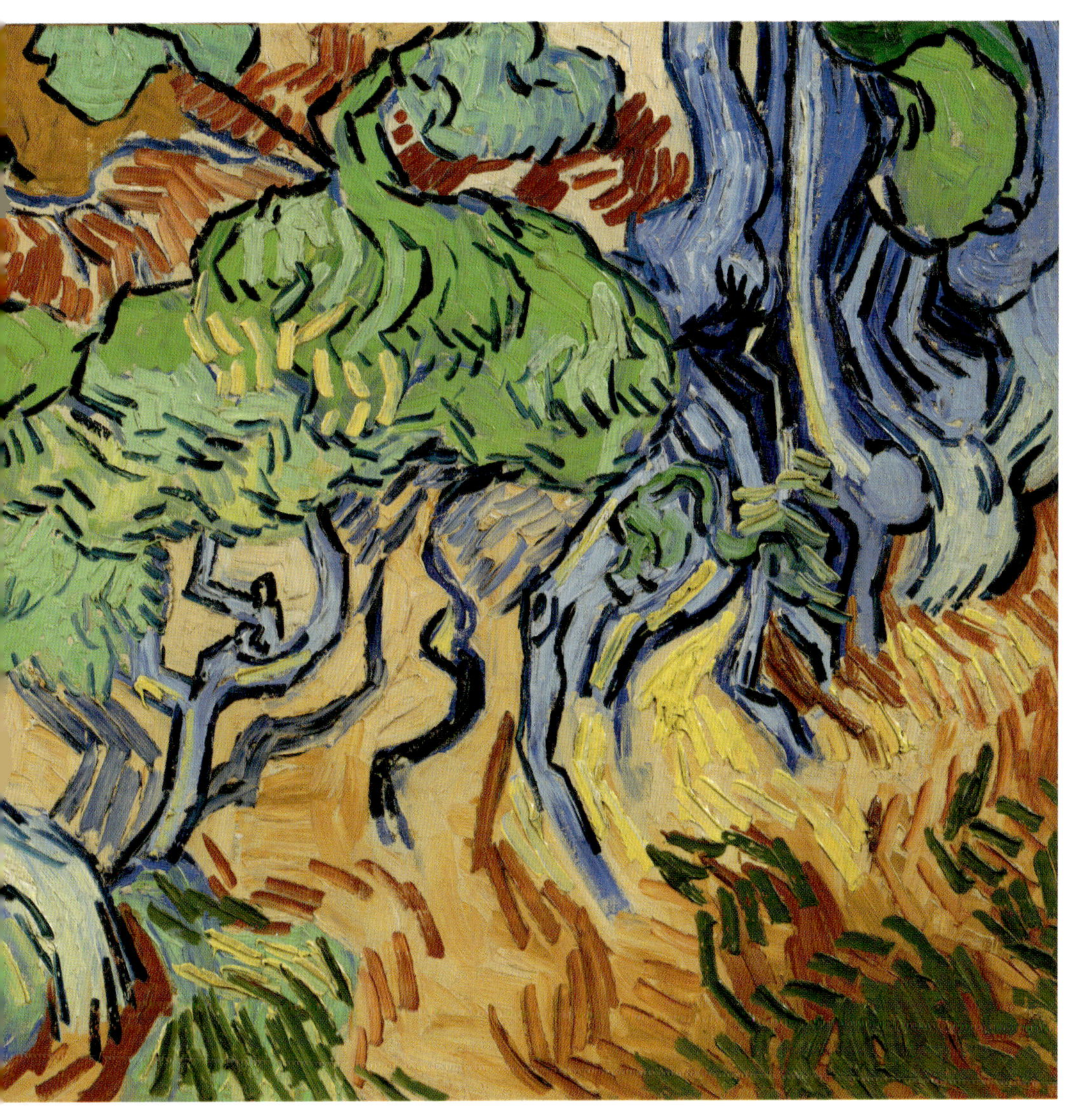

[9] *Tree Roots and Trunks*
Auvers-sur-Oise, July 1890
Vincent often chose a double-square-sized canvas for his panoramic landscape paintings of fields. In this work, he employed the format to suggest a steep bank. Stylized tree forms with writhing contours envelop the brightly coloured canvas. Although the painting has the appearance of a decorative screen, the feverish outlines of the blue trees and the expressive brushstrokes lend the image an unsettling character.

Although Vincent relished the quiet beauty of man-made spaces, it was often the dramatic forms of the trees in the landscape that he sought to capture in paint. In his mind, individual trees even assumed the role of people: 'Those trees, they were superb, there was a drama in each *figure* I'm tempted to say, but I mean in each tree' (381) [10]. Trees struggling against the extreme forces of nature became the subject of a number of paintings and drawings [11] [12]. These trees, buffeted by storm-force winds, were associated in his poetic mind with human emotions: 'Yes, for me the drama of a storm in nature, the drama of sorrow in life, is the best' (381). In some of his very late paintings of woods, the psychological drama that he wished to convey resulted in images of a distinctly sinister character. The woods ceased to be the benign settings of his youth – now they became almost threatening places that transmitted anxiety [13].

While in some of his representations of trees Vincent merely alluded to ideas about anthropomorphism, in one famous example, dating from 1882 [14] [15], the connections between tree and human figure were made more explicit.

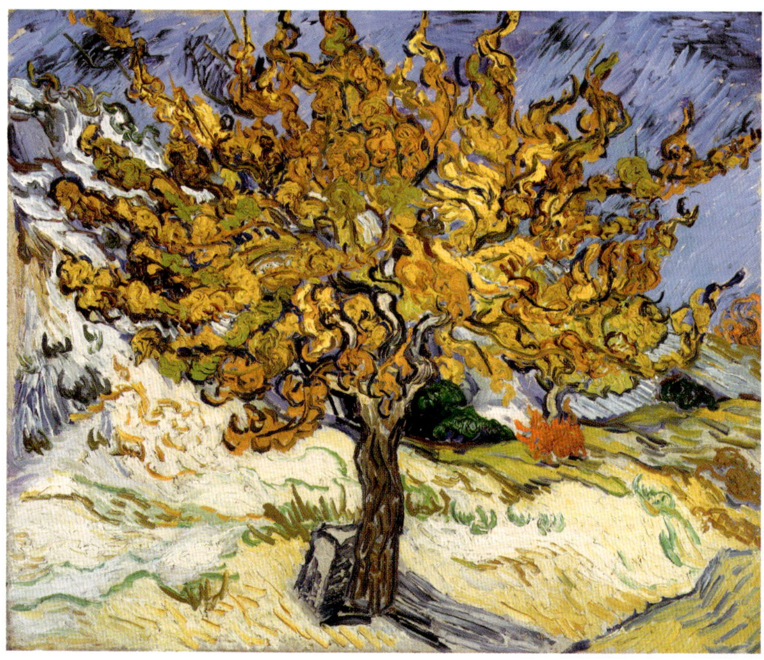

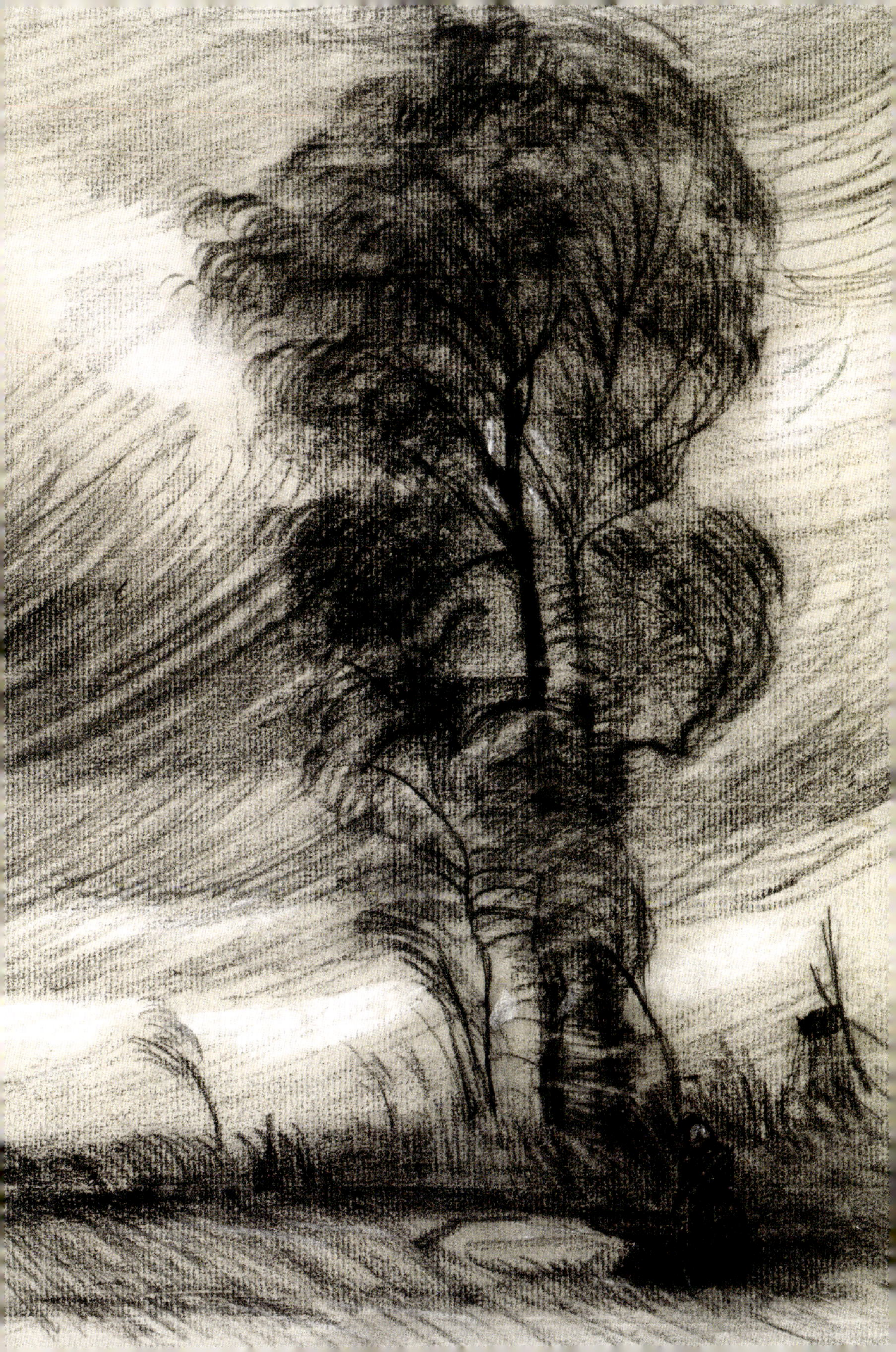

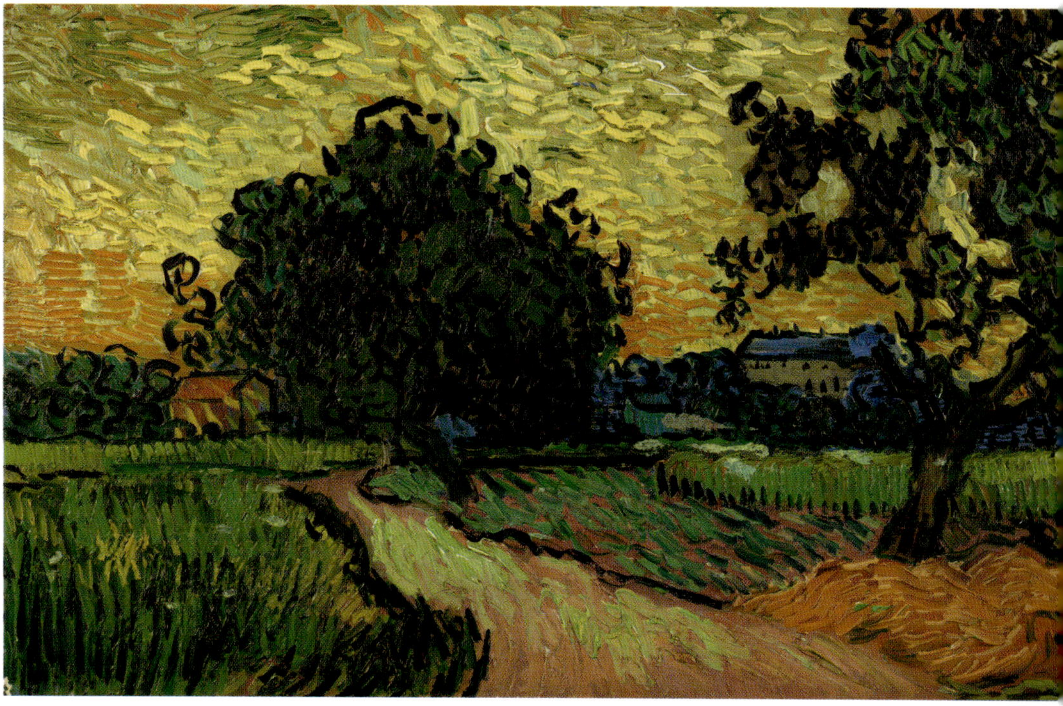

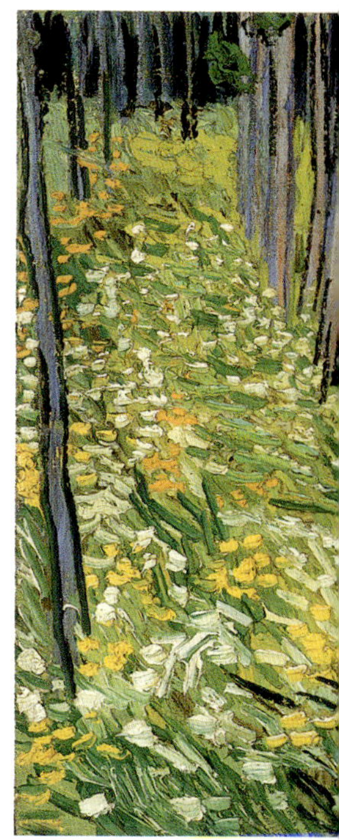

[13] *Couple Walking
between Rows of Poplars*
Auvers-sur-Oise, June 1890
Vincent used the double-square
format to great effect in this
painting to represent a wide expanse
of woodland, and the dominant
verticals of the tree trunks lend the
composition a frieze-like character.
In spite of the brightly coloured
elements of the tree trunks, flowers
and grass, the painting has a
distinctly claustrophobic character.
While the mood could have been
lifted by the addition of one of
Vincent's favourite elements,
a pair of lovers, the figures have
in fact taken on the appearance of
somewhat disconcerting manikins.

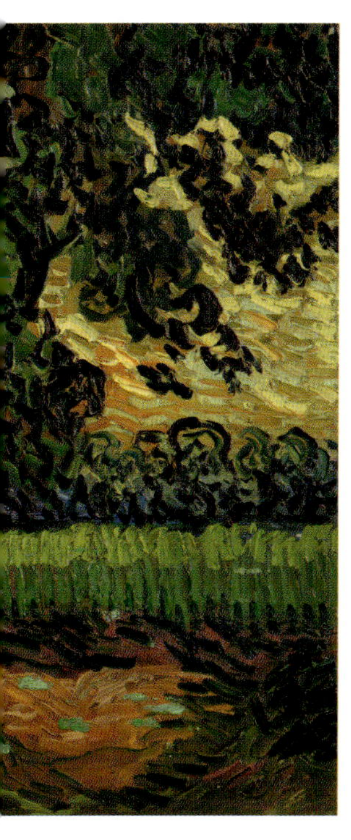

LEFT
[12] *Landscape at Twilight*

Auvers-sur-Oise, June 1890

Vincent described the key features
of this brooding landscape in
a letter to Theo: 'Finally a night
effect – two completely dark pear
trees against yellowing sky with
wheatfields' (891). In terms of
technique, the painting reveals
his admiration for the bold, skilful
brushwork of seventeenth-century
Dutch painters such as Frans Hals
(*c.* 1580–1666). The canvas was
completed quickly, probably
in just one session – a method
Vincent particularly favoured.

LEFT

[12] *Landscape at Twilight*
Auvers-sur-Oise, June 1890
Vincent described the key features
of this brooding landscape in
a letter to Theo: 'Finally a night
effect – two completely dark pear
trees against yellowing sky with
wheatfields' (891). In terms of
technique, the painting reveals
his admiration for the bold, skilful
brushwork of seventeenth-century
Dutch painters such as Frans Hals
(*c.* 1580–1666). The canvas was
completed quickly, probably
in just one session – a method
Vincent particularly favoured.

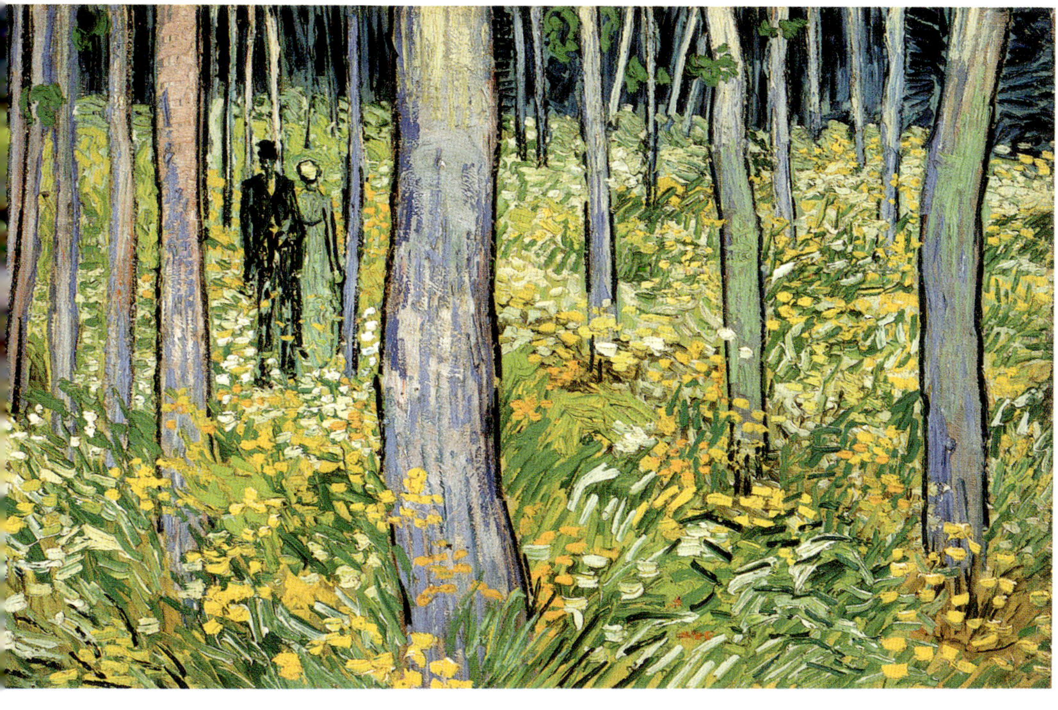

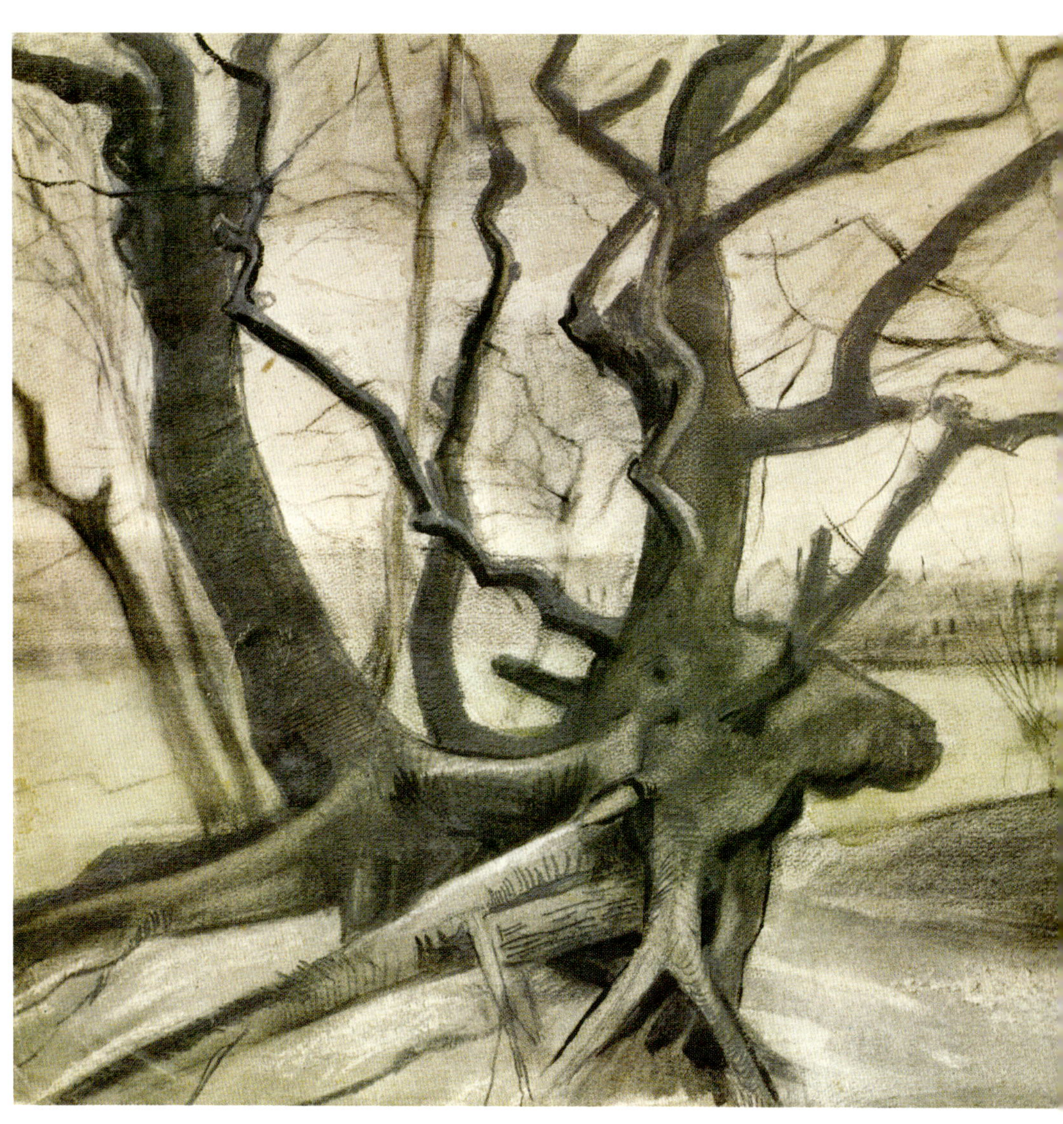

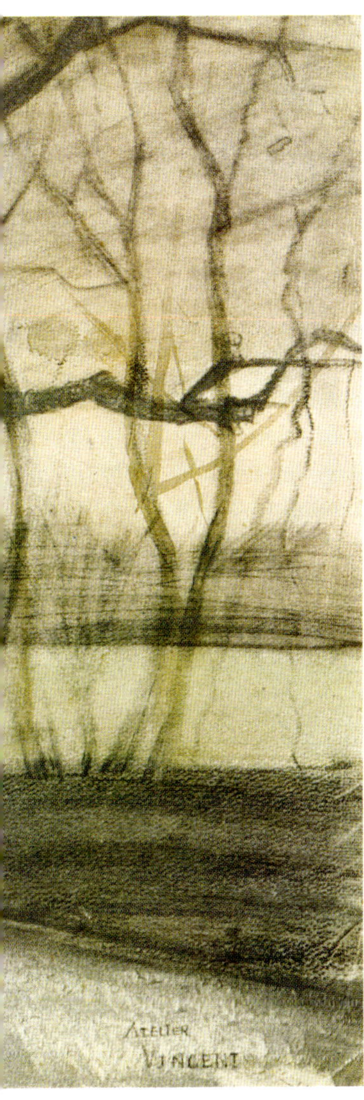

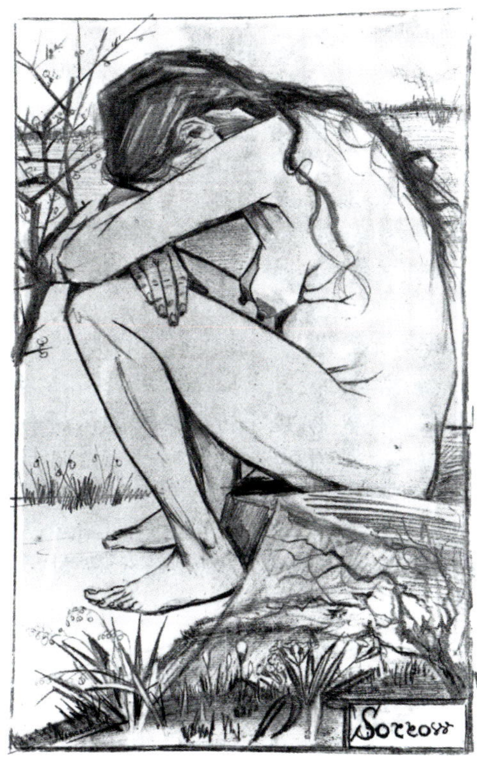

LEFT

[14] *Study of a Tree*
Pencil, chalk, ink, watercolour
on wove paper
The Hague, April 1882
This is one of Vincent's most
accomplished drawings of a
tree, and one of his earliest as
a professional artist. Being 'half
torn up by the storm' (222), the
tree became a symbol of survival.
It was a version of this image that
he described as being imbued with
the same emotions as his drawing
of an abandoned woman, *Sorrow*.

ABOVE

[15] *Sorrow*
Pencil and black chalk
on laid paper
The Hague, April 1882
Vincent was greatly influenced in
his early figure compositions by the
English illustrators whose works
he collected. Like them, he wished
for his drawings to have a strong
emotional impact on the viewer
and believed that in this drawing of
a sad, lonely figure he had achieved
a small measure of success: 'I want
to make drawings that *move* some
people. Sorrow is a small beginning'
(249). The model for this work was
his mistress, Clasina ('Sien') Maria
Hoornik (1850–1904), who had
experienced many hardships in life.

He viewed his powerful drawing of a tree 'fervently rooting itself' (222) as analogous to his poignant portrayal of a grief-stricken female nude . Vincent believed that both images epitomized the need for endurance in the face of adversity, a quality evident in all living things: 'I wanted to express something of life's struggle, both in that white, slender female figure and those gnarled black roots with their knots' (222). Underlining the thematic link between the two works, the drawing of the woman, inscribed with the title *Sorrow*, also contains tree imagery: the forlorn figure is sitting on a tree stump, while beside her a contorted branch is coming into blossom.

Early in his career, Vincent wrote to Theo, summing up his overall aim as an artist: 'I want to reach the point where people say of my work, that man feels deeply and that man feels subtly' (249). It could be argued that the depth and subtlety of his feelings, while evident in much of his *oeuvre*, were most clearly expressed when he employed symbolism explicitly [16] [17]. In these works he endeavoured to reveal the universal in the particular. Thus, for him, a sower was a symbol of regeneration, while a tree in blossom became a harbinger of hope. Overall, trees took on a symbolic role for Vincent, resulting in drawings and paintings of enigmatic beauty.

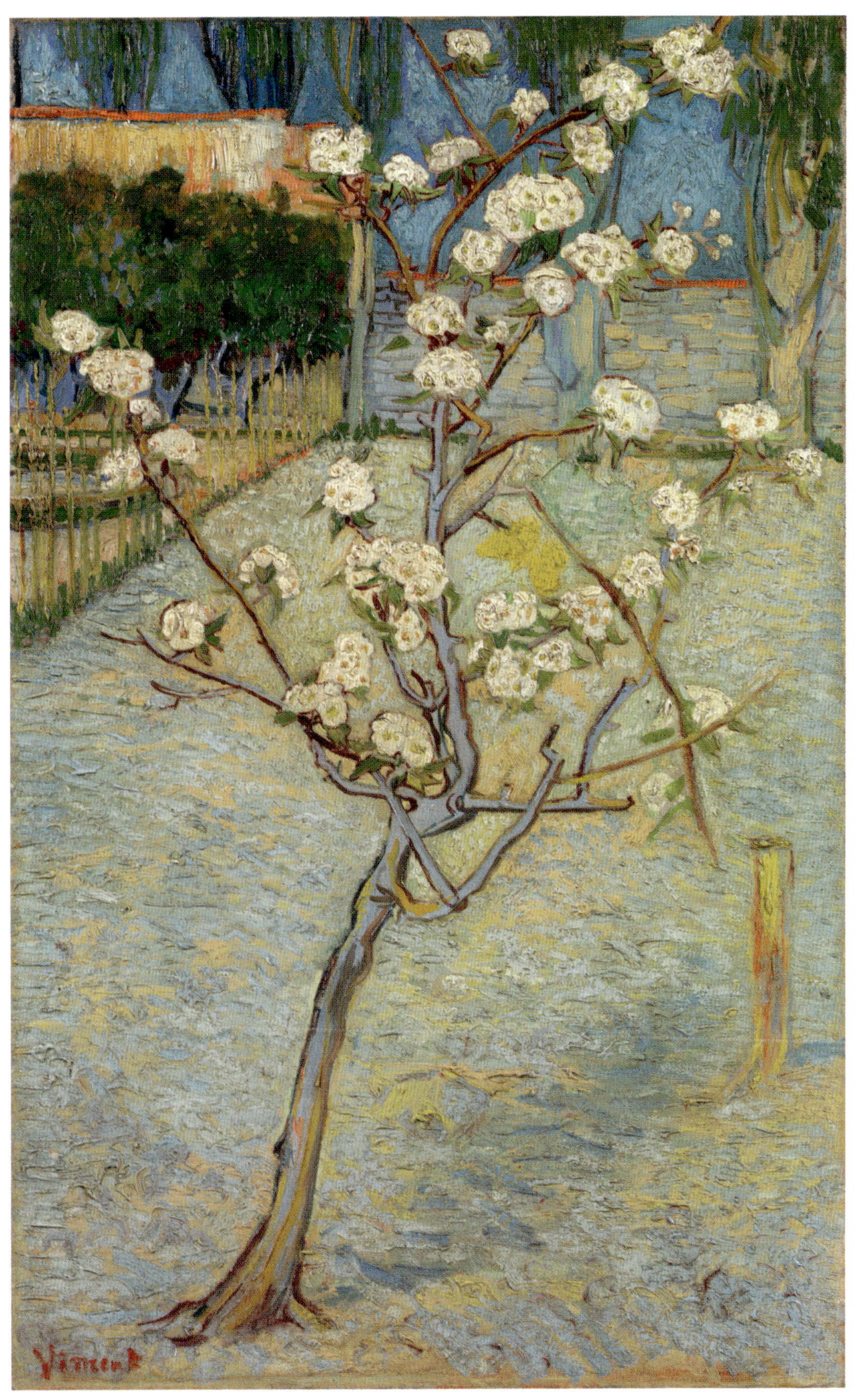

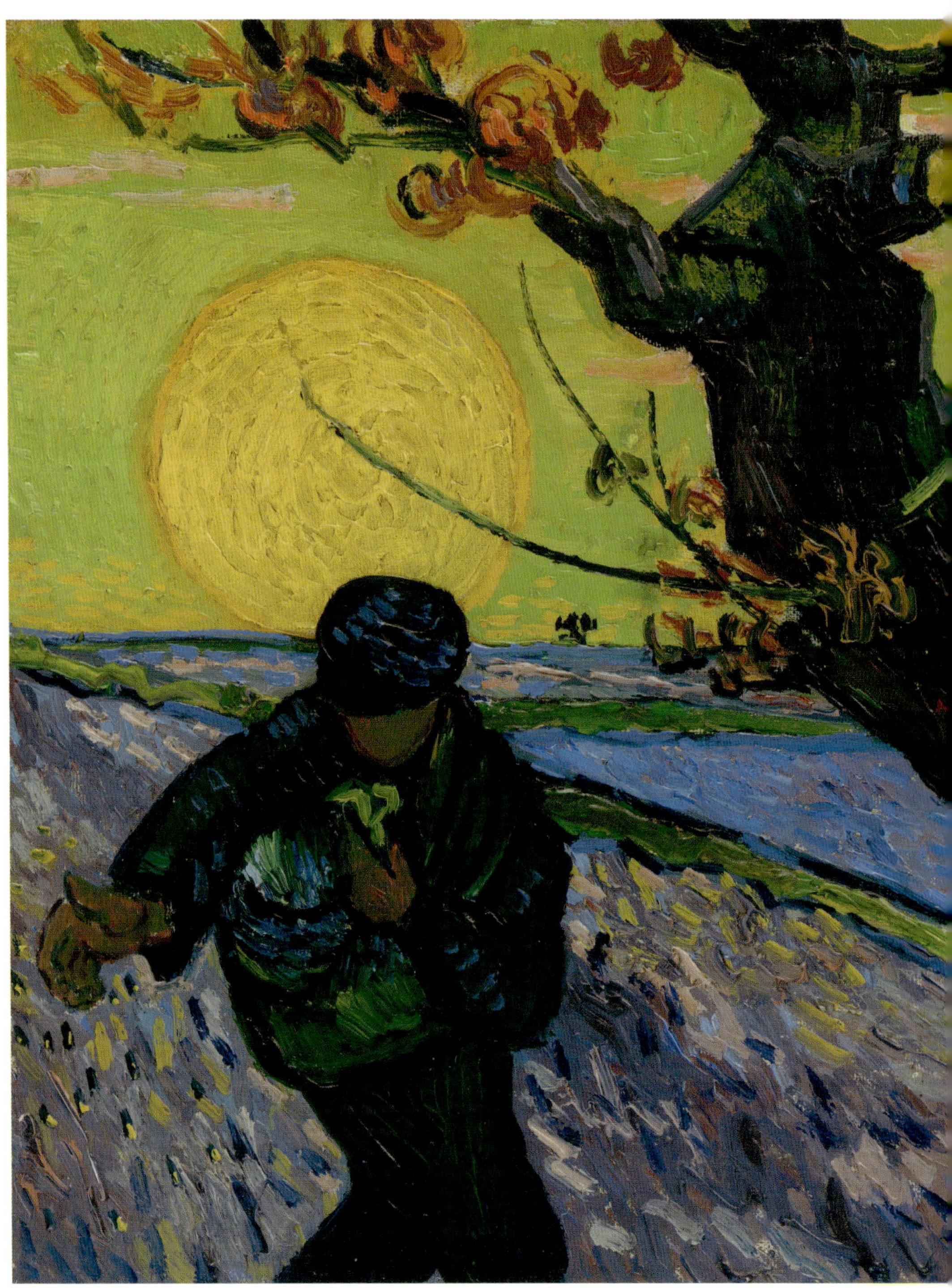

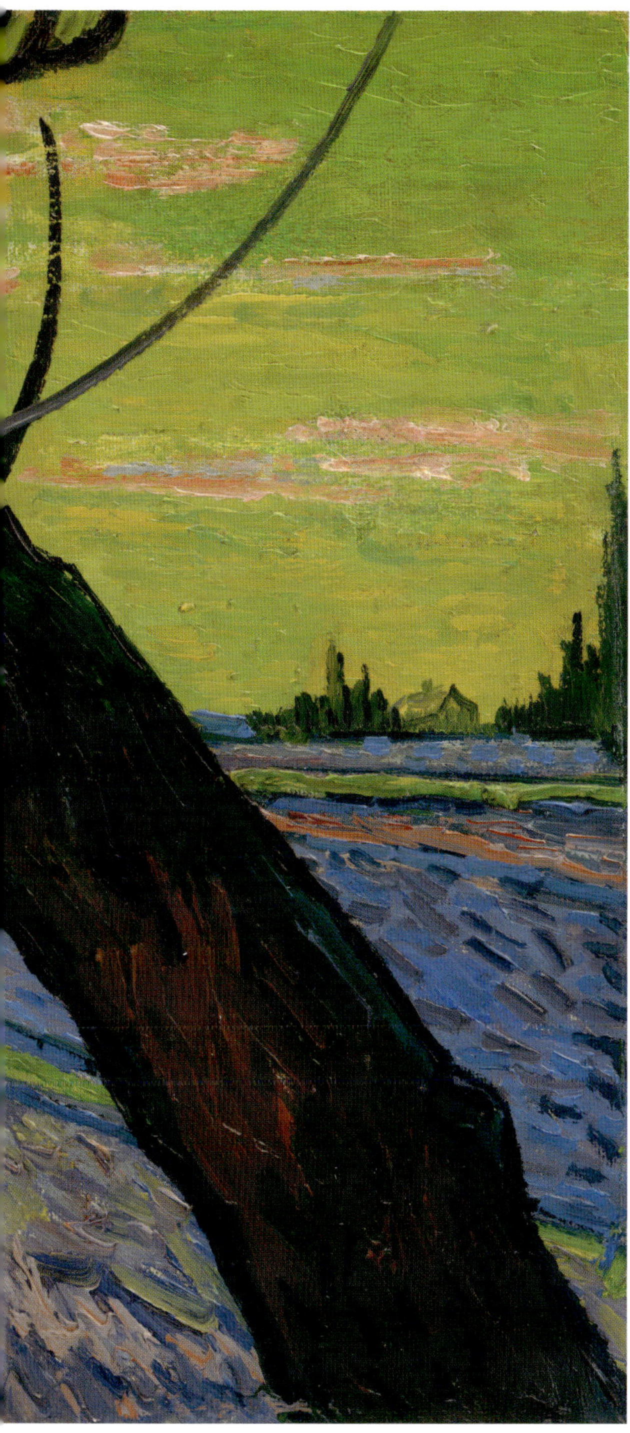

[17] *The Sower*

Arles, November 1888

In this emblematic work, Vincent achieved a powerful synthesis of various motifs that he had previously painted directly from nature: a pollard willow tree, a sower casting seed, a wide field and an enormous sun in a vast sky. Painting from memory, he created one of his most poetic improvisations, with the flat, colourful design owing much to the influence of Japanese woodblock prints. As for the quasi-religious overtones of the image, Vincent had previously written of his 'yearnings for the infinite of which the sower, and the sheaf, are the symbols' (628). This small canvas almost assumes the role of an icon, with the sun forming a halo for the sanctified peasant, who is bringing new life to the earth.

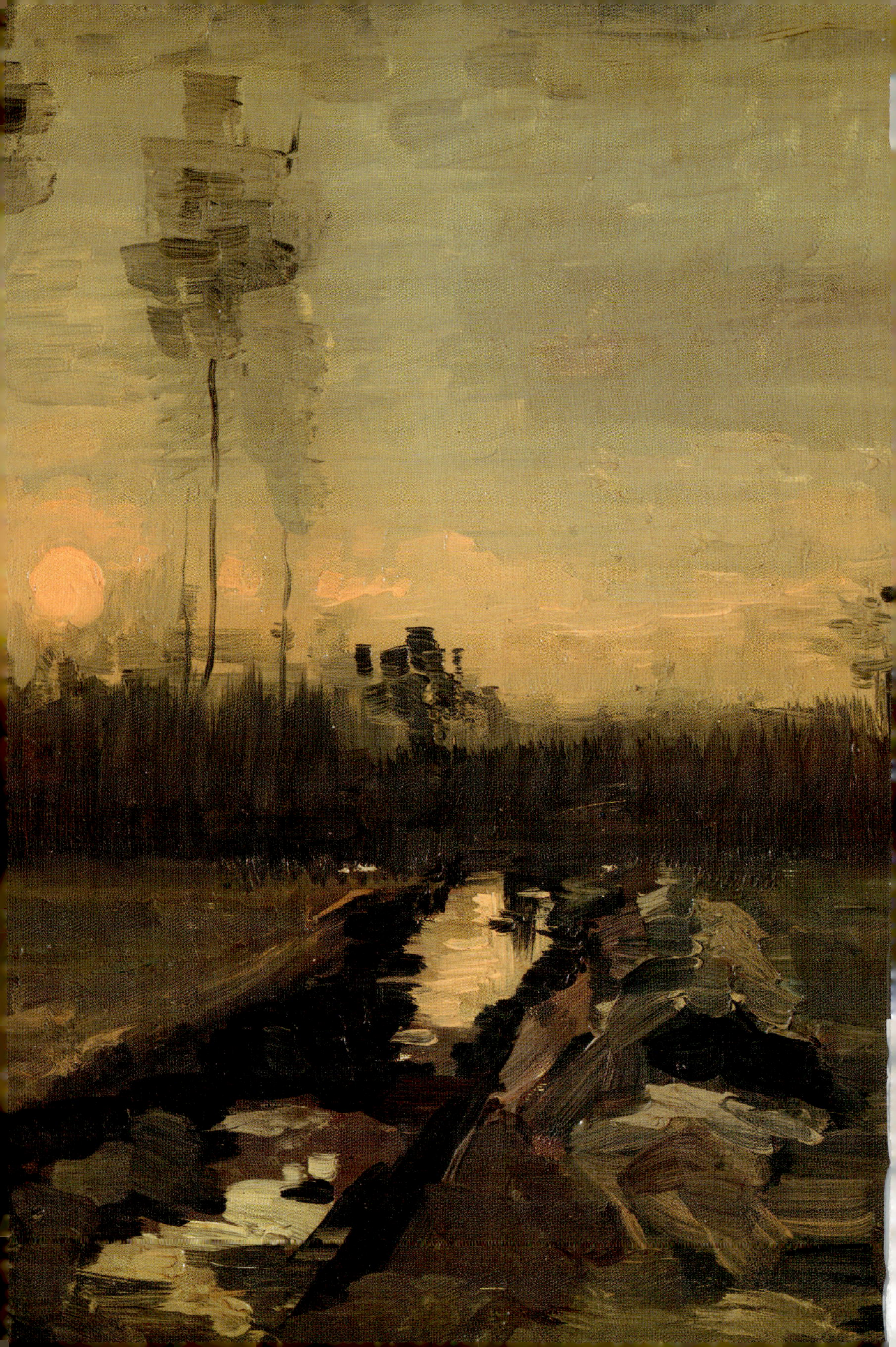

CHAPTER 2

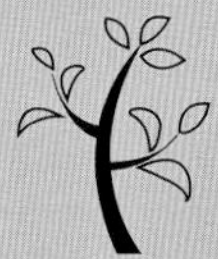

Vincent's Dutch Trees

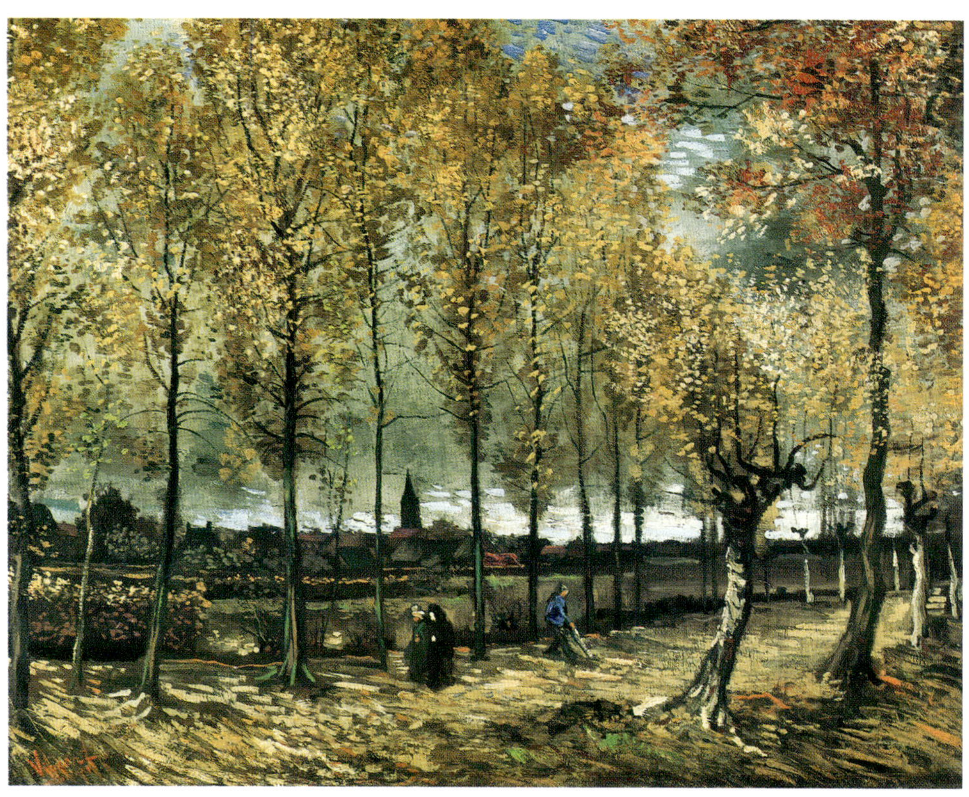

PAGE 32
[19] *Landscape at Dusk* (detail)
Nuenen, April 1885
An example of Vincent's virtuosity
with oil paint, this image of a damp
landscape is suffused with the
amber light of dusk. The broadly
applied, luscious pigment gives the
picture the aspect of an oil sketch.
In fact, during his Dutch period,
Vincent advocated the quick, bold
application of paint: 'Paint in one
go, as far as possible in one go' (535).
The quivering foliage of the line of
trees was achieved with the greatest
economy of means – just a few
horizontal strokes of a broad brush.

ABOVE
[18] *Avenue of Poplars*
Nuenen, November 1885
Vincent admired the graceful beauty
of poplar trees during the autumn
months. On one occasion he wrote
of being 'surrounded by slender
poplars whose yellow leaves one
could hear falling' (402).

'Imagine, right then, an avenue of tall poplars with the autumn leaves...'

From April 1881 until the end of November 1885, Van Gogh lived and worked in the Netherlands. For three years, he developed his skills as an artist in a number of villages, concentrating on rural subject matter, including woods and tree-lined roads. The poplars planted along the country lanes and on the boundaries of fields provided motifs for many of his early drawings and paintings [18]. In terms of colour and atmospheric effects, the tree paintings often exhibit a muted, tranquil quality redolent of the Dutch landscape. Walking along the quiet lanes and exploring the beech woods, Vincent felt at ease in his quest to become a painter of nature: 'Rarely of late has the stillness, nature alone, so appealed to me' (369).

When extolling the beauty of tree species in his drawings and paintings, Vincent endeavoured to combine two differing philosophies of visual art that were prevalent at that time. He acknowledged wholeheartedly that a work of art should reflect a painter's feelings and emotions, and might hint at literary and symbolic parallels, but he also wished to base his art on close, accurate observations of nature and everyday life. Thus his work in the Netherlands, and elsewhere, can be interpreted as a synthesis of a Romantic and poetic approach to painting with one that stresses realism: 'Half Romantic, half realistic – a combination of styles I find not unsympathetic' (360) [19].

In fact, Vincent's career as an artist began not in his native land but in Belgium. Until 1879 he had been working as a lay missionary in the Borinage, the coal-mining district in the south, near the town of Mons. While not a talented preacher, he proved popular with the miners and their families due to his kindness. However, he became over-zealous in his duties and started to experience symptoms of extreme stress and depression. Eventually he was dismissed from his post and his father began to make arrangements for his admission to an asylum. Fortunately, Vincent recovered during a brief recuperative stay with his parents in the Netherlands, and he insisted on returning to the Borinage village of Cuesmes, where, in August 1880, he took the momentous decision to become an artist.

He justified his decision to Theo by reminding him of the great passion for painting he had developed during his employment by the major art dealers Goupil & Cie between 1869 and 1876. Indeed, Vincent confessed that, since then, he had often felt 'homesick for the country of paintings' (155). Understandably, given his vulnerability and previous lack of direction, Vincent's relatives had grave doubts as to whether he could become an accomplished artist. However, he possessed a good knowledge of art history and the art market, and was extremely well read; what's more he displayed great intelligence and was trilingual. Once he started drawing exercises from the instruction manuals devised by the French artist Charles Bargue (1826–1883), the novice artist believed that he had found a new focus in his life, and perhaps even a cure

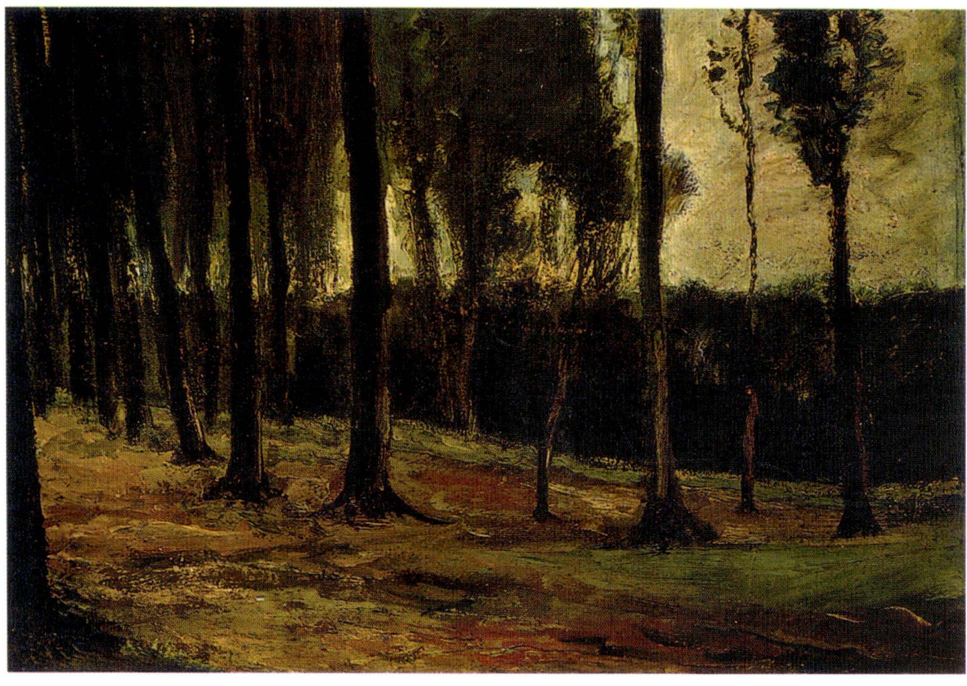

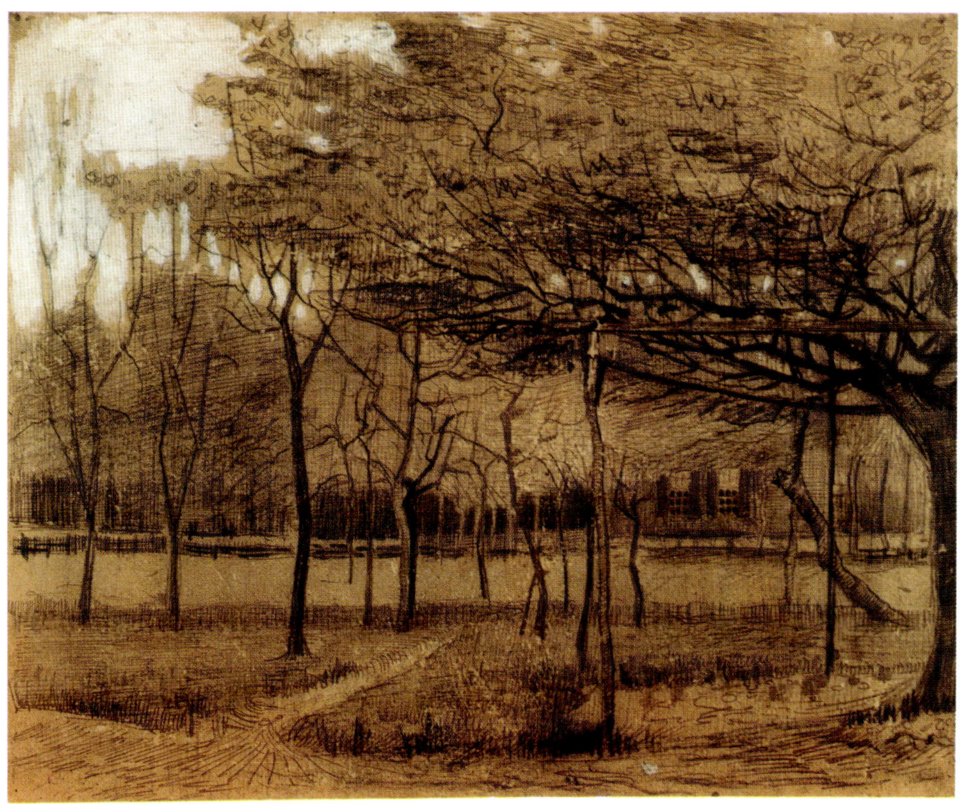

for his mental health problems: 'If only I can go on working, I'll recover' (156). However, while he had ceased to be a missionary, he pursued his new calling with a similar evangelic zeal. Over the next ten years, his work proved an outpouring of creativity unique in the history of European painting, eventually leading to his becoming one of the most famous artists of all time [20].

The cramped quarters he rented in Cuesmes, and later in Brussels, were not ideal for his new life as an artist and so in April 1881 he decided, somewhat reluctantly, to return to the Netherlands, where he was to live with his parents for the next nine months. His father's parsonage was located in Etten, a typical North Brabant rural village. Here, Vincent concentrated on improving his drawing skills and powers of observation [21]. His perception of his surroundings, including the woods, orchards and the parsonage garden, had been heightened, he believed, due to his new commitment to drawing:

[21] *Orchard*
Etten, June 1881
Vincent relished the calm atmosphere of orchards, where he could prepare detailed drawings of trees close to his studio and living quarters. The orchards also possessed a certain formality in terms of planting that appealed to his sense of pictorial composition.

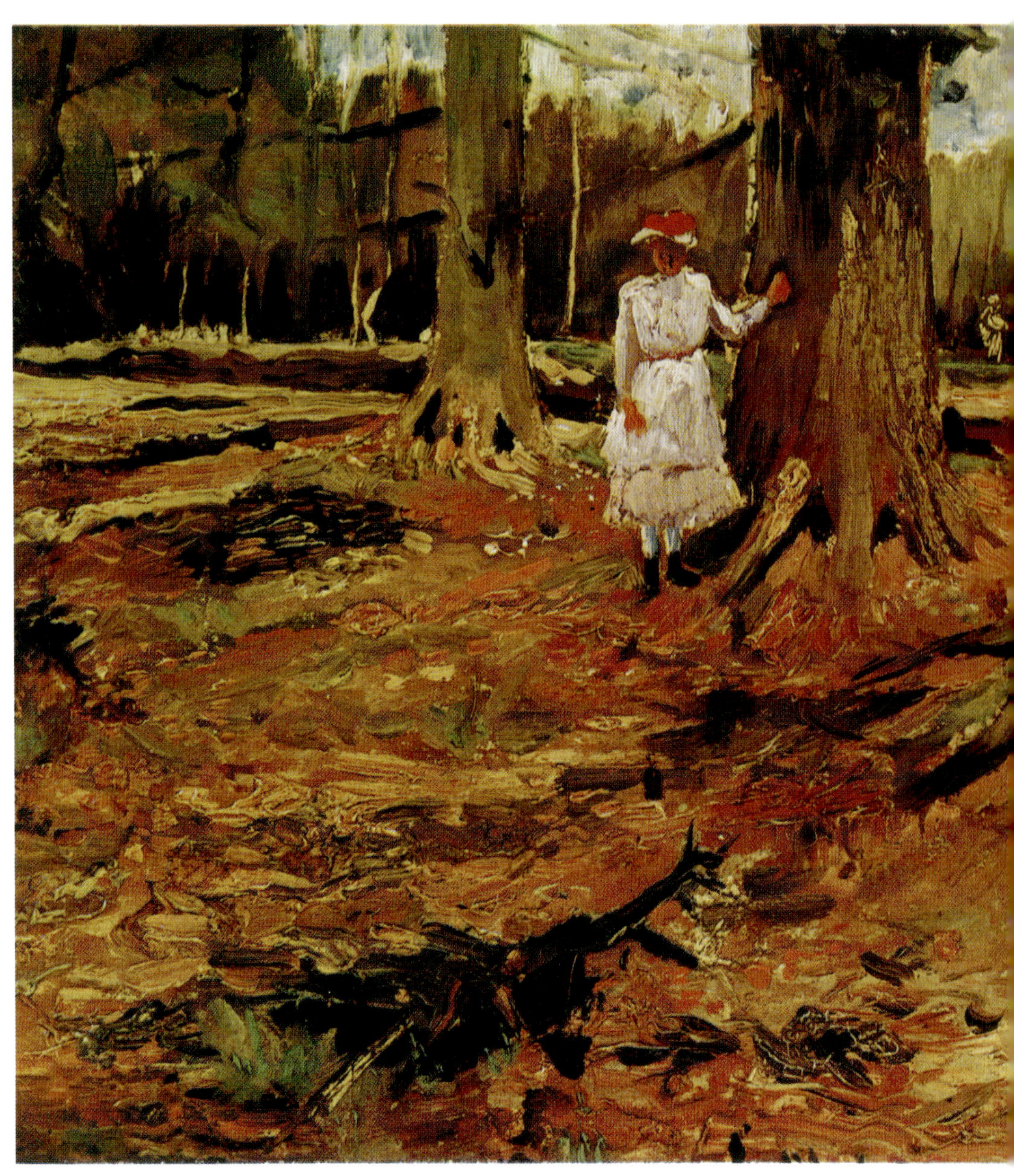

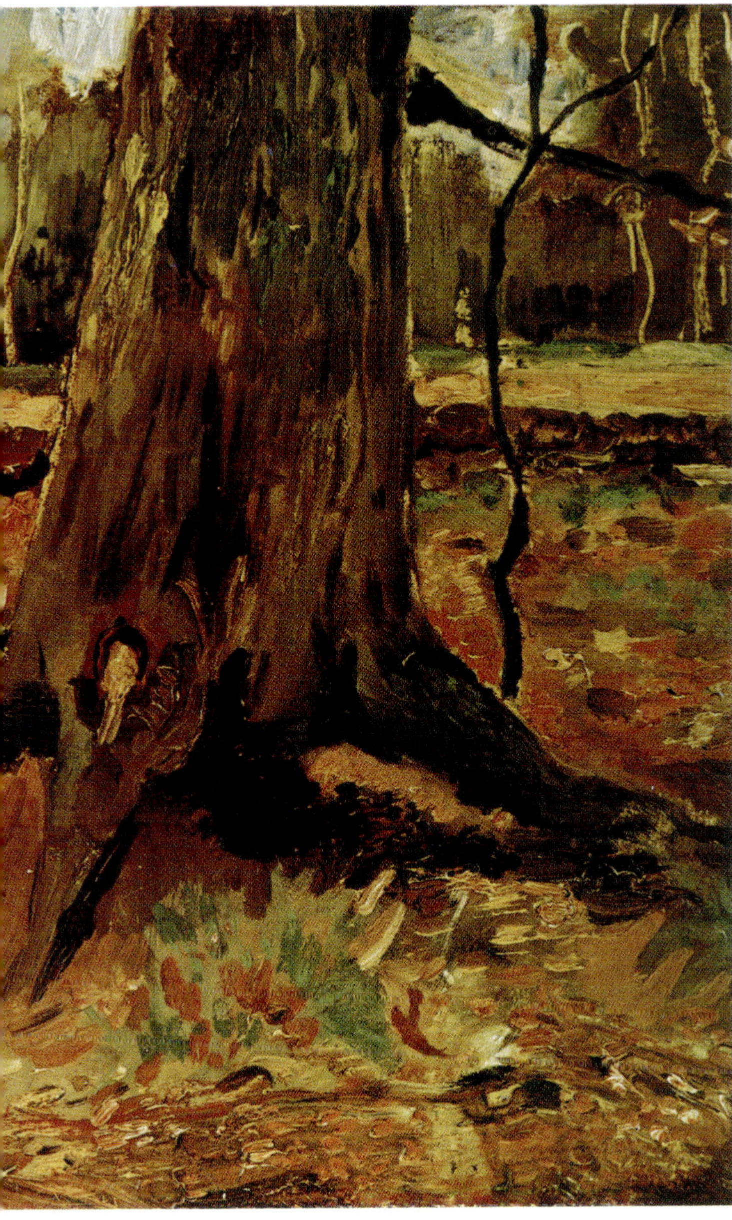

[22] *Girl in a Wood*
The Hague, August 1882
Vincent delighted in the visual
richness of the groundcover he
encountered in the beech woods:
'For there's no carpet imaginable
as splendid as that deep brown-red
in the glow of autumnal evening'
(260). Although this early work,
with the graceful figure of a girl,
shows the progress he had made
with oil paint, Vincent wrote of
the difficulties he had to overcome
in its creation. Above all, he wished
to create the impression 'that one
can breathe and wander about
in it – and smell the woods' (258).

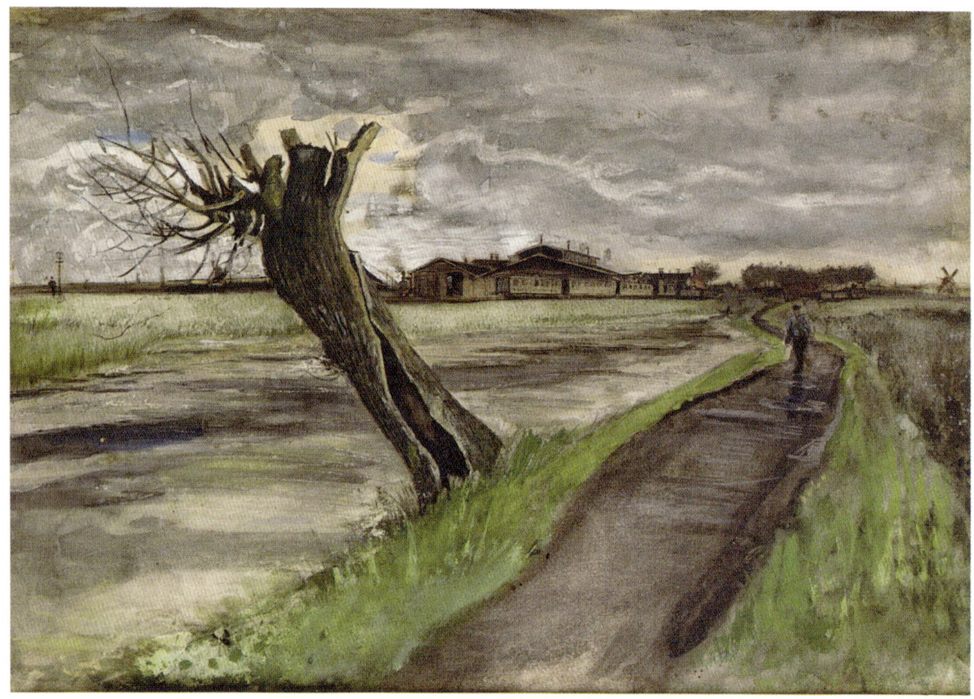

[23] *Pollard Willow*
Watercolour, gouache, pen and ink
on paper, laid down on board
The Hague, July 1882
In typical anthropomorphic fashion,
Vincent described this pollard
willow as being 'all alone and
melancholy' (251). He was intrigued
by the elaborate textures and subtle
colour tones of the dead tree's bark.
His 'sombre landscape' of 'that old
giant' (252) was, he believed, the
best watercolour he had produced
in The Hague. Interestingly, in 1648,
Rembrandt had etched an image of
a dead pollard tree, *St. Jerome beside
a Pollard Willow*, and Vincent may
have been familiar with it.

'Now I see things with a different eye from the time when
I wasn't yet drawing' (157).

In December 1881, Vincent moved to The Hague and
began to experiment with the oil paint medium, encouraged
by his cousin's husband, Anton Mauve (1838–1888).
Famous for his atmospheric landscapes, Mauve was the
leading painter of the Hague School, a prominent group
of Dutch artists active between 1870 and 1888, who stressed
the naturalistic representation of landscapes and urban
scenes. Hague School paintings were noteworthy for their
distinctive misty tones of grey and gold. They were very
influential among artists and collectors in the Netherlands
and Scotland, and also admired by Van Gogh, which is
evident in some of his early work. He considered himself
extremely fortunate to have an artist as accomplished as
Mauve agree to give him lessons in drawing, watercolour
and oil painting.

Mauve's new pupil seemed appreciative at first, stating
that the renowned Dutch painter had taught him 'to see

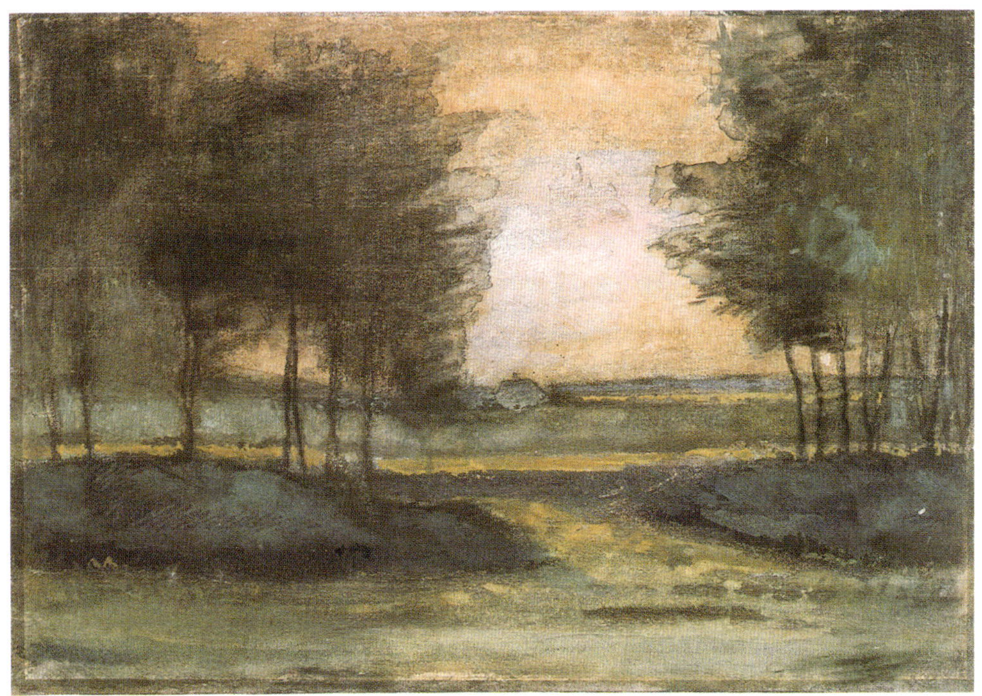

so many things I didn't see before' (193). But soon conflicts
arose. Vincent disputed the value of drawing from plaster
cast sculptures and Mauve criticized his pupil's bohemian
lifestyle. As a result, the two artists ceased to communicate.

During his stay in The Hague between December 1881
and September 1883, Vincent often walked through the
Haagse Bos, a large cluster of beech woods close to the
city. It was here that he composed some of his earliest oil
paintings of trees [22]. The beech trees not only made him
aware of subtle colour effects but also stimulated his literary
tendencies: 'Out of the ground shoot young beech trees
that catch the light on one side – are brilliantly green there
– and the shaded side of those trunks a warm, strong black-
green' (260). On his excursions into the countryside that
surrounded the city he sometimes encountered individual
trees that resonated with his visual imagination. His
watercolour of a large pollard willow reveals his fascination
with this characteristically Dutch tree and also shows the
value of his studies with Mauve in this difficult medium [23].

[24] *Landscape in Drenthe*
Black chalk, ink and watercolour
on laid paper
Drenthe, Autumn 1883
In Drenthe Vincent was repeatedly
reminded of the diaphanous
landscapes created by one of his
favourite artists, Jean-Baptiste-
Camille Corot (1796–1875). He
also admired the Frenchman's
drawings and engravings of trees.
In this watercolour, which is perhaps
directly influenced by Corot,
Van Gogh sought to encapsulate
the 'vaporous atmosphere' of the
landscape, which was enveloped
'in a spectrum of delicate greys' (402).

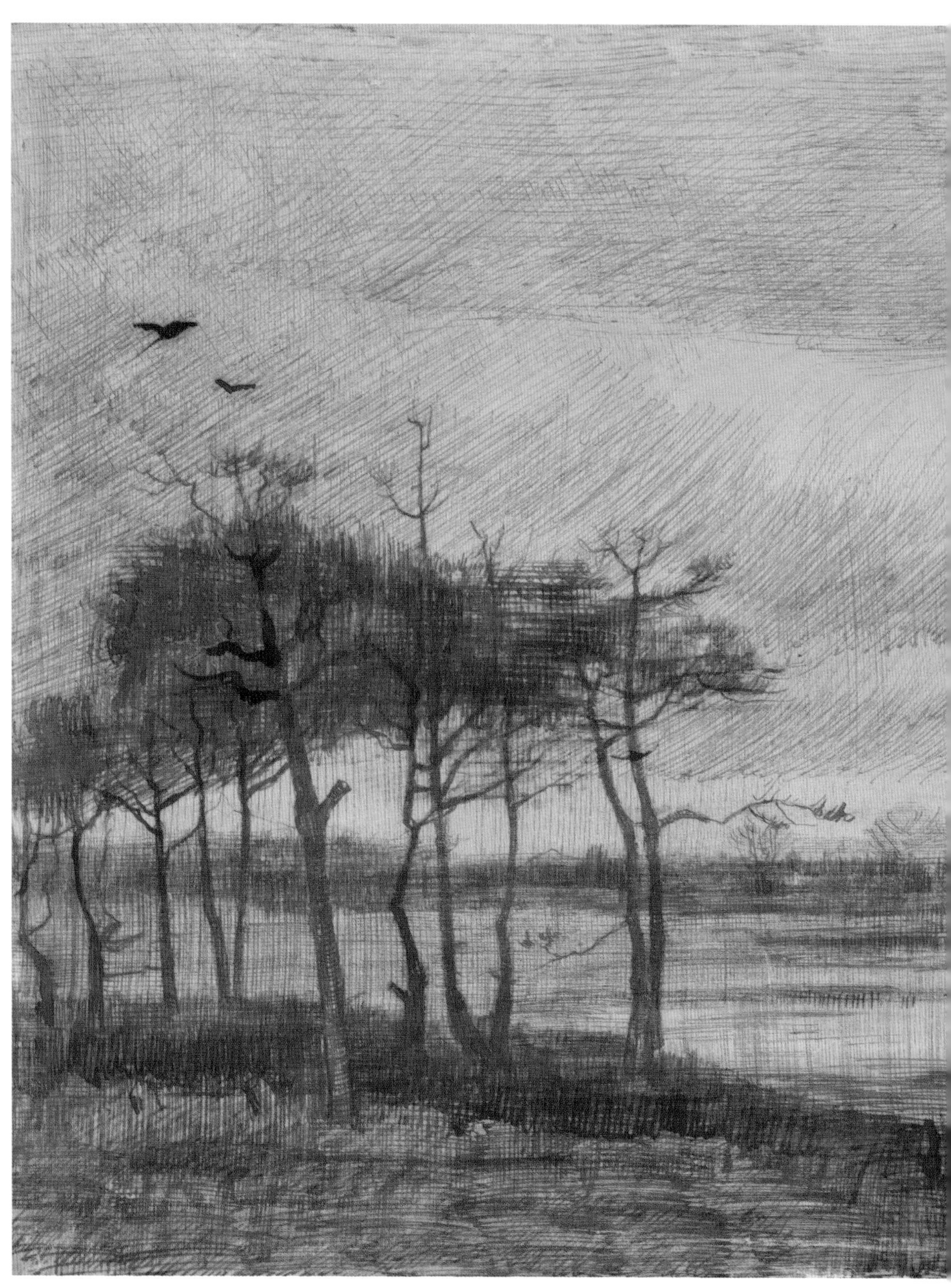

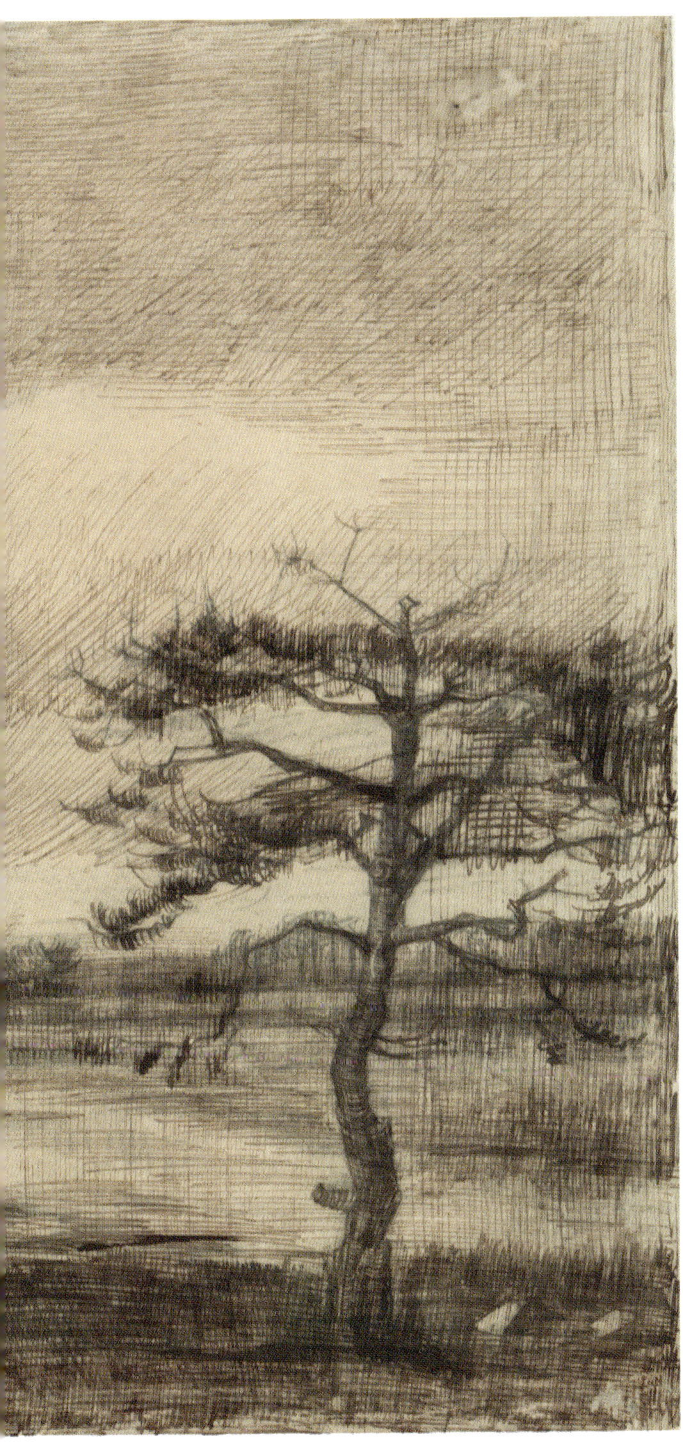

[25] Pine Trees in the Fen
Pencil, pen and brush in brown
ink on wove paper
Nuenen, April 1884
The pine trees, which he had so
admired during his childhood in
Zundert, are shown here almost
in silhouette, and the large expanse
of sky and the watery marshland
have been captured by swift
cross-hatching. In a letter to his
artist friend Van Rappard, Vincent
explained that he had attempted
'somehow to render the effect
of light and shade' (441).

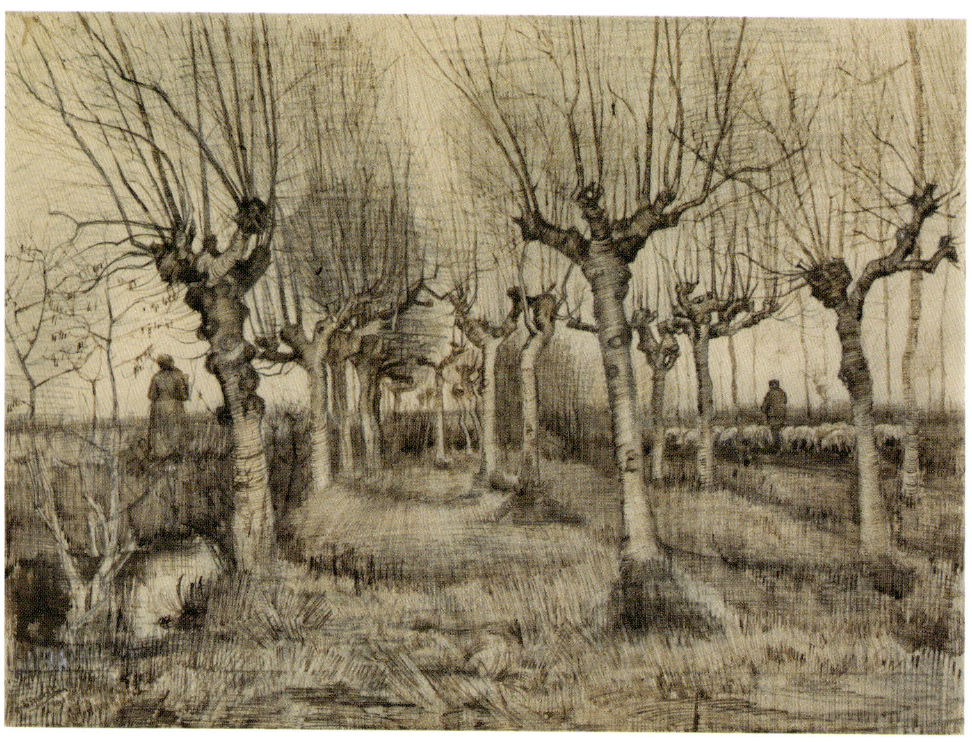

[26] *Pollard Birches*
Pencil, pen in brown ink (originally
black), heightened with opaque white
watercolour, on wove paper
Nuenen, March 1884
A copse of pollard trees provided the
dramatic setting for this drawing
with its strong sense of perspective.
The annual pollarding of willows
and birches produced bursts
of thin branches that formed a
distinctive feature of rural Brabant.
Vincent traced the gnarled forms
of the regimented trees with dense
networks of intersecting pen lines.
Despite the addition of the pastoral
figures, the drawing possesses a
certain gloomy intensity.

Having lived almost two years in the city environment,
Vincent left The Hague for Drenthe, the most underpopulated
and least-developed province of the Netherlands. Located
in the northeast of the country on the border with Germany,
Drenthe had long been a magnet for Dutch painters,
including Mauve and Vincent's friend Van Rappard, whom
he had met in Brussels. Landscape artists in particular were
attracted by the province's heath and moorland, its woods
and picturesque farms. Given Vincent's rural upbringing,
these features immediately cast a spell on him, as did the
region's restful atmosphere: 'A silence, a mystery, a peace'
(402). Although the cost of living was much lower than in
The Hague, and Vincent was entranced by the landscape
and its delicate, limpid light, he was to explore the villages
of Drenthe for only three months [24]. He completed some
interesting pieces of work, but increasingly suffered from
severe depression, which he feared might again become
debilitating. His father sent him money and suggested that,

for health reasons, Vincent should return to North Brabant
to live with his parents, this time in the village of Nuenen
(where his father had been appointed as the local parson).
He did so, and while this was a pragmatic solution to his
health and pecuniary problems, for Vincent it represented
a personal defeat; the independence he had achieved, albeit
subsidized by Theo, had evaporated. But the landscape and
trees of North Brabant soon invigorated him, resulting in
ink drawings and oil paintings of great subtlety [25].

The pollarding of willows and birches was a common
activity in the surrounding rural environment. Practised
since medieval times, this form of pruning, when applied
to young trees, promotes their health and prolongs their life.
At the time, the new branches were harvested for fuel or for
fences. Birches, when heavily pollarded and truncated, lent
themselves to elaborate exercises in draughtsmanship [26].
Later, when living in the south of France, Vincent wrote to
his mother confiding that he missed the birches 'which were
so beautiful in Nuenen' (788).

Small groups of beech trees provided colourful subjects close
to the parsonage, especially when observed in autumn [27].

[27] *Autumn Landscape
with Four Trees*
Nuenen, November 1885
Although Van Gogh admired
the colours displayed by trees in
autumn, he sometimes despaired
of ever being able to capture their
beauty in paint: 'Everything is
already bronze…and so beautiful
that one's imagination always
falls short of it' (381). The group
of four trees that dominate this
composition grew along the lane
at the bottom of the parsonage
garden. The juxtaposition of the
stark pollard tree with the three
specimens in full leaf is striking.

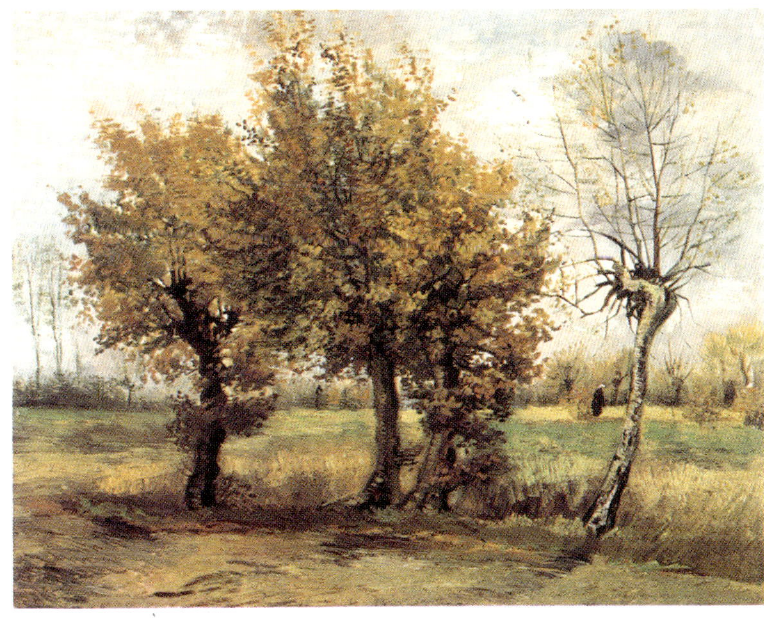

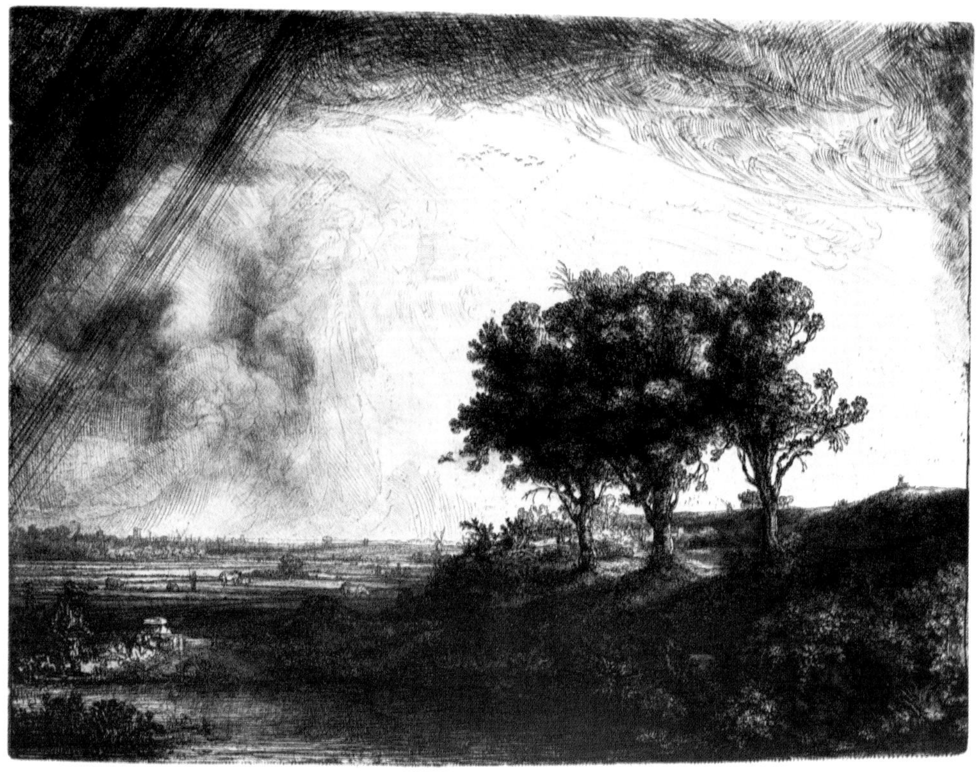

Vincent's interest in this type of composition may have been influenced by Rembrandt's famous etching *The Three Trees*, created in 1643 [28]. Vincent did not have to walk far in order to draw and paint trees: the parsonage garden displayed intriguing effects – particularly in the winter months – which he could study in complete privacy. The result was a series of drawings and paintings in which complex patterns of bare or snow-covered tree branches are dominant features [29] [30].

Vincent's drawings and paintings of poplar trees have immortalized the tree-lined lanes and avenues of North Brabant. In fact, due to the evocative nature of these images and Vincent's international fame, the lanes are now included in the Dutch Heritage list of protected sites. Poplar trees, spaced evenly along roads and edges of fields, have long been employed as windbreaks and, being fast-growing, as a natural means of improving drainage. For Vincent, the poplar

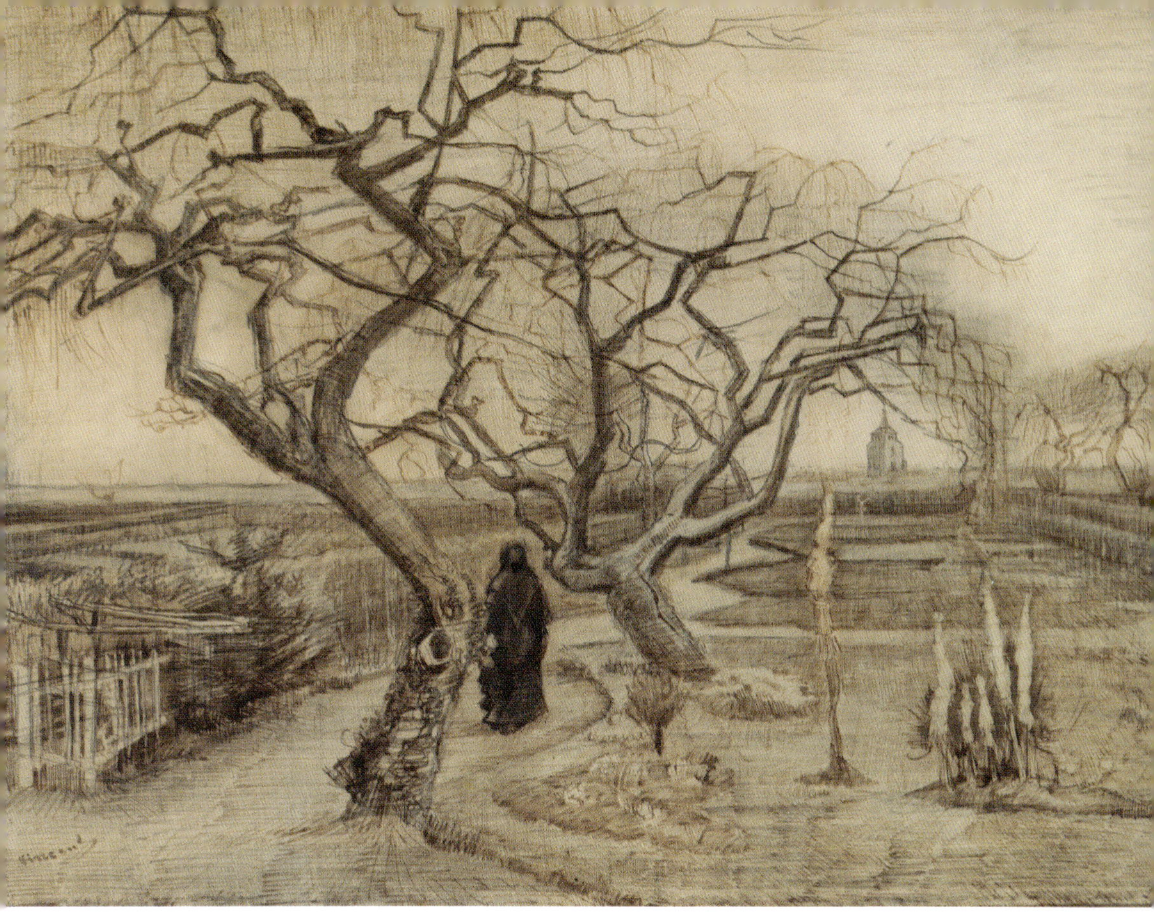

avenues had a timeless, enigmatic quality, which
he successfully captured on canvas and in ink drawings
[31] [32]. By adding small figures to these compositions,
he conveyed the verticality and dominant scale of the slender
trees within the flat landscape [33]. Vincent was a great
admirer of the landscape paintings of Meindert Hobbema
(1638–1709), in particular his acknowledged masterpiece,
The Avenue at Middelharnis (1689), which he had studied closely
in the National Gallery in London. Vincent's canvases of
straight avenues dominated by serried ranks of tall trees
can be seen, therefore, as part of a long tradition in Dutch art.

Early on in his Dutch period, Van Gogh had concluded that,
given his life experiences, he felt obliged – almost duty-
bound – 'to leave a certain souvenir in the form of drawings
or paintings in gratitude' (371). Art lovers can only be grateful
that his depictions of Dutch trees form part of this memento.

[29] *Winter Garden*
Pencil and pen in brown ink
(originally black) on wove paper
Nuenen, March 1884
Two large trees with elaborate
configurations of interlaced
branches dominate this garden
scene. Vincent explained to Van
Rappard that by adding a shrouded
figure he had hoped to create a
ghostly effect – a mood further
emphasized by the mysterious
derelict church on the horizon.

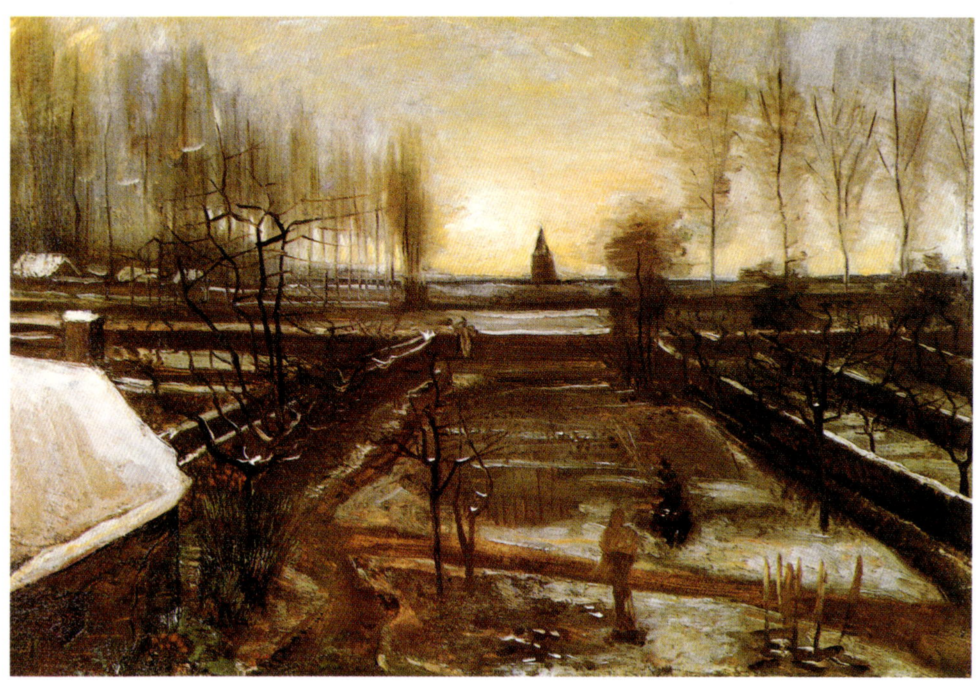

[30] *The Parsonage Garden
at Nuenen in the Snow*
Nuenen, January 1885
The vantage point for this winter
scene appears to have been an
upstairs window of the parsonage.
To the left is the roof of the
outbuilding that Vincent used
as a studio at the beginning of 1884.
The garden's snow-topped hedges
act as perspective lines leading to
the old tower, which provides a
dramatic vanishing point. The light
covering of snow on the garden's
trees is conveyed by deft touches
of white paint, and a line of feathery
trees forms a delicate screen on
the horizon.

[31] *Avenue of Poplars at Sunset*
Nuenen, October 1884
Vincent often felt that avenues
of trees were most appealing
to him 'when the peculiar light
of autumn evenings does its work'
(264). In selecting a vertical format
for this painting he accentuated
the thin, regularly spaced nature
of the poplars. As in other works,
he combined the setting sun and the
solitary figure into a symbolic design.

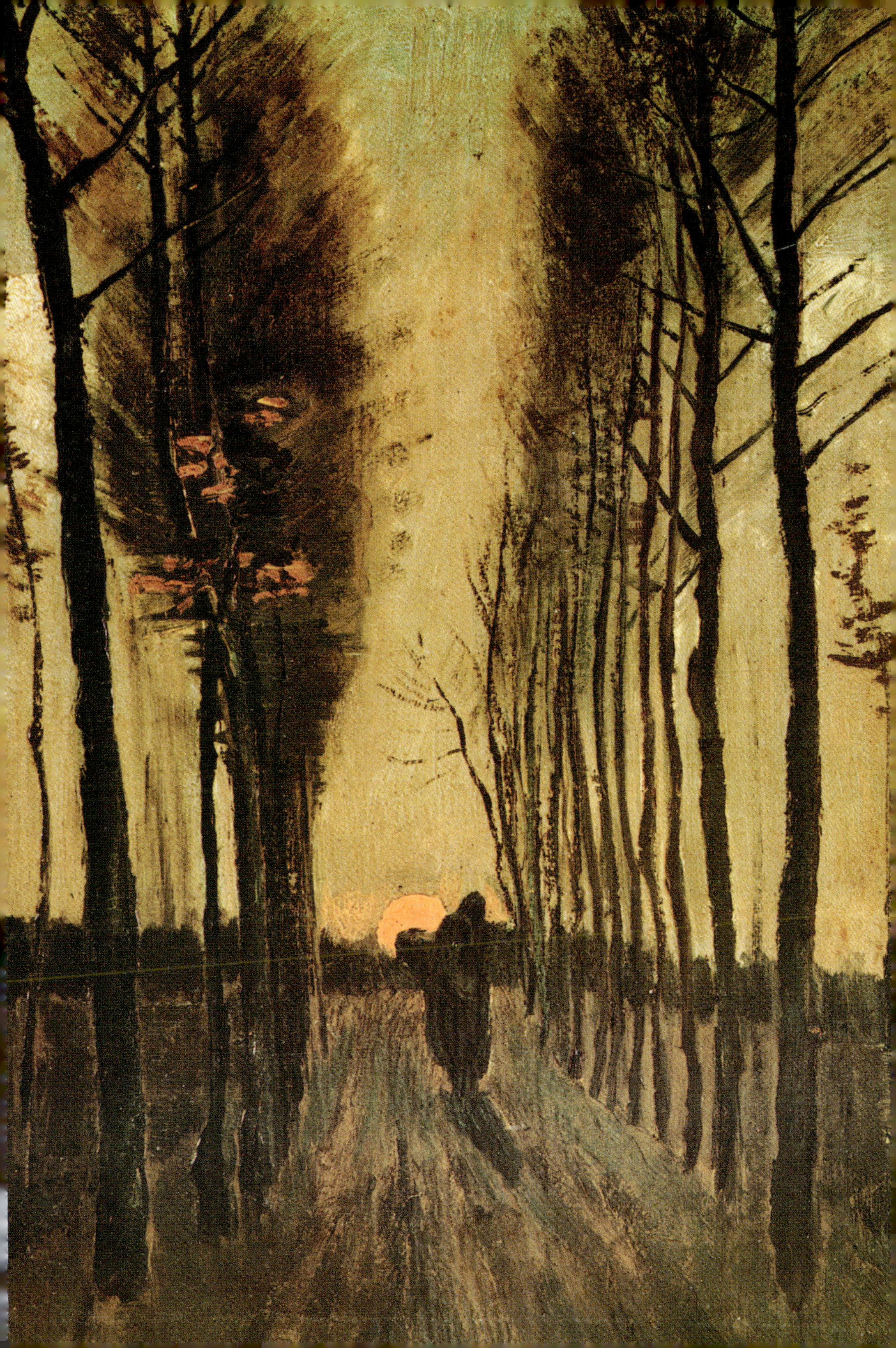

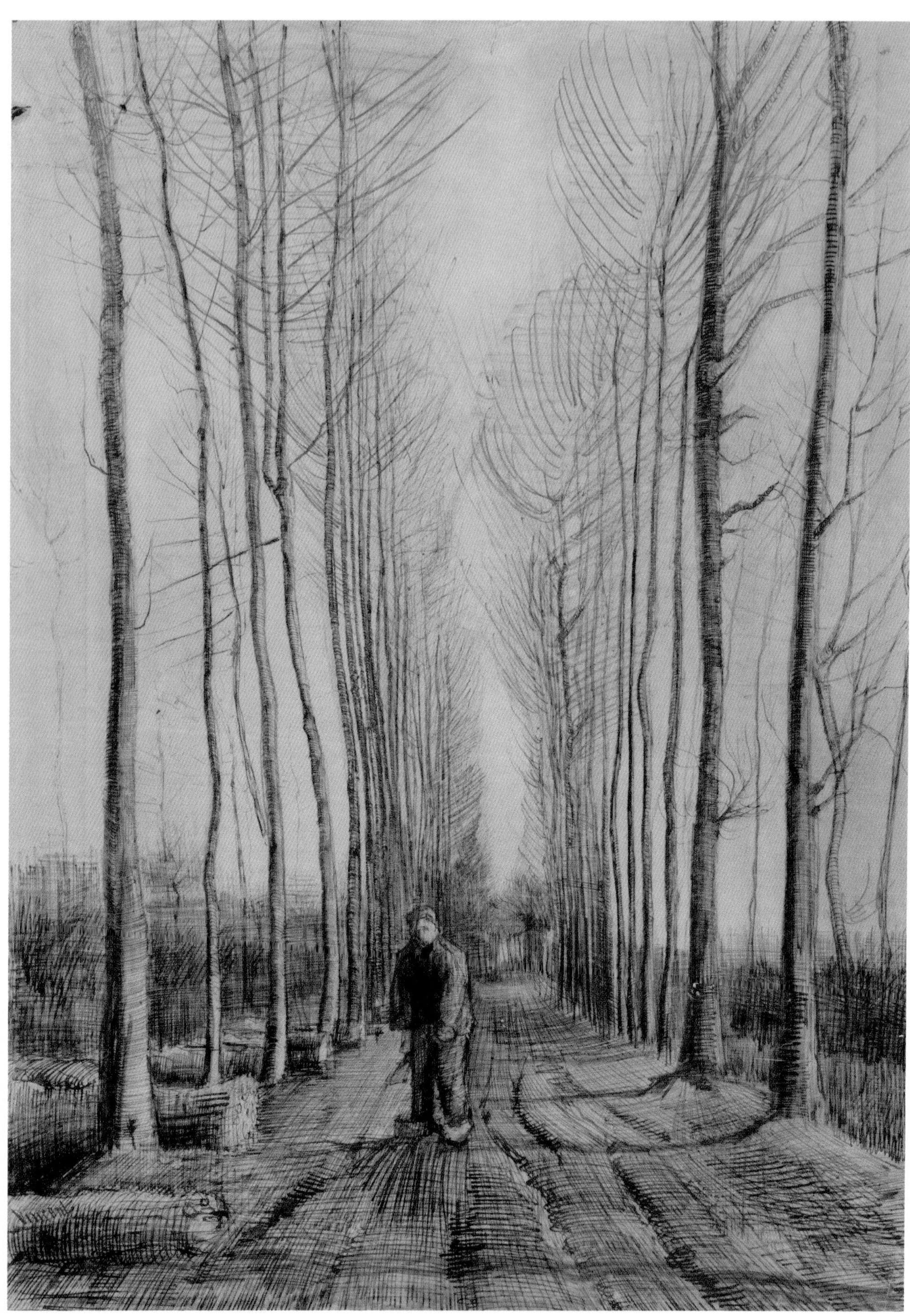

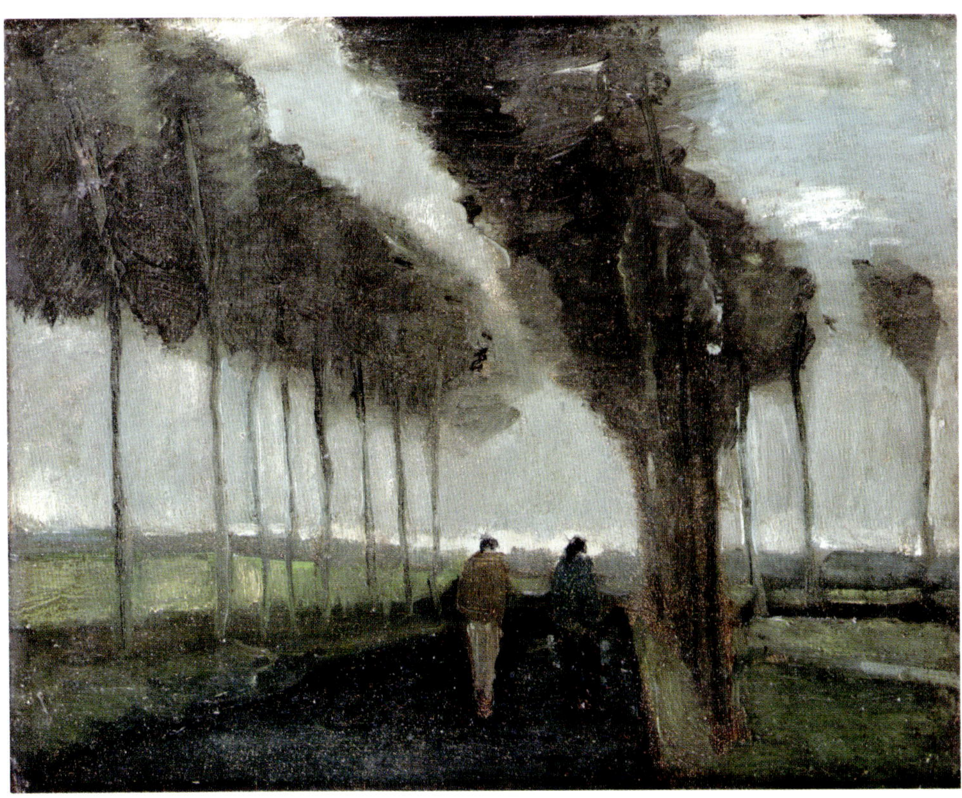

OPPOSITE
[32] Avenue of Poplars
Pencil and pen in brown ink
(originally black) on wove paper
Nuenen, March 1884
Although he was attracted by
gnarled, sculptural trees as subject
matter, Vincent was also captivated
by the spare elegance of 'thin spindly
poplars' (333) in the straight rural
lanes of Nuenen. The linear planting
of this water-loving species gave
Vincent an opportunity to hone
further his skills in perspective.
He used thin pencil lines sensitively
to suggest the delicate nature of
the bare tree branches.

ABOVE
[33] Country Lane with
Two Figures
Nuenen, October 1885
The trees give a vertical rhythm
and a strong sense of space to this
evocation of a rural lane. The muted
tones of green and brown, and the
small scale of the two figures in the
flat landscape, contribute to the
contemplative mood of the painting.

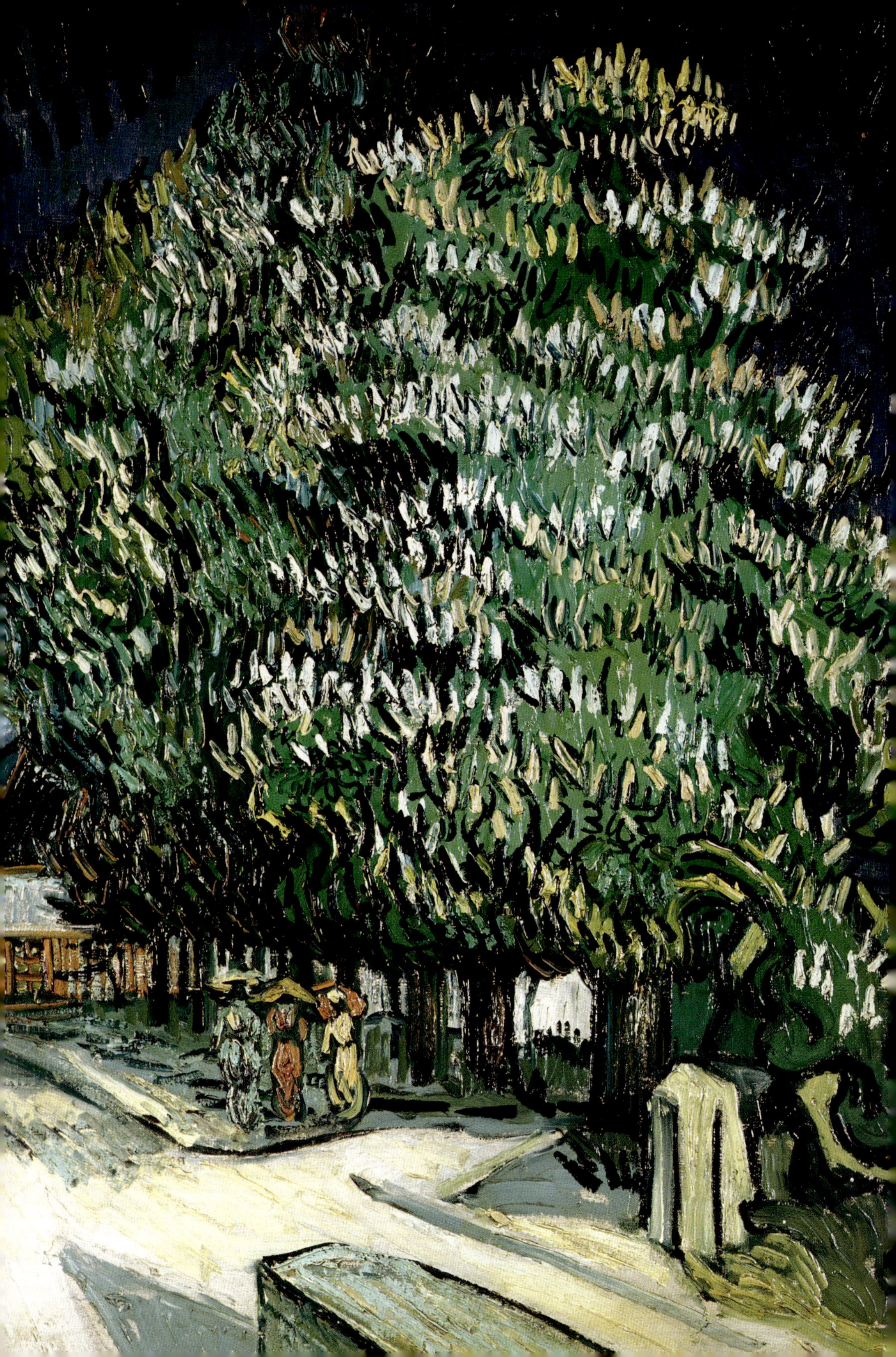

CHAPTER 3

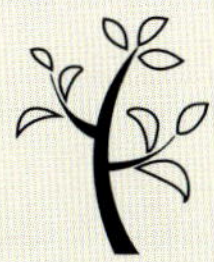

Vincent's Townscape Trees

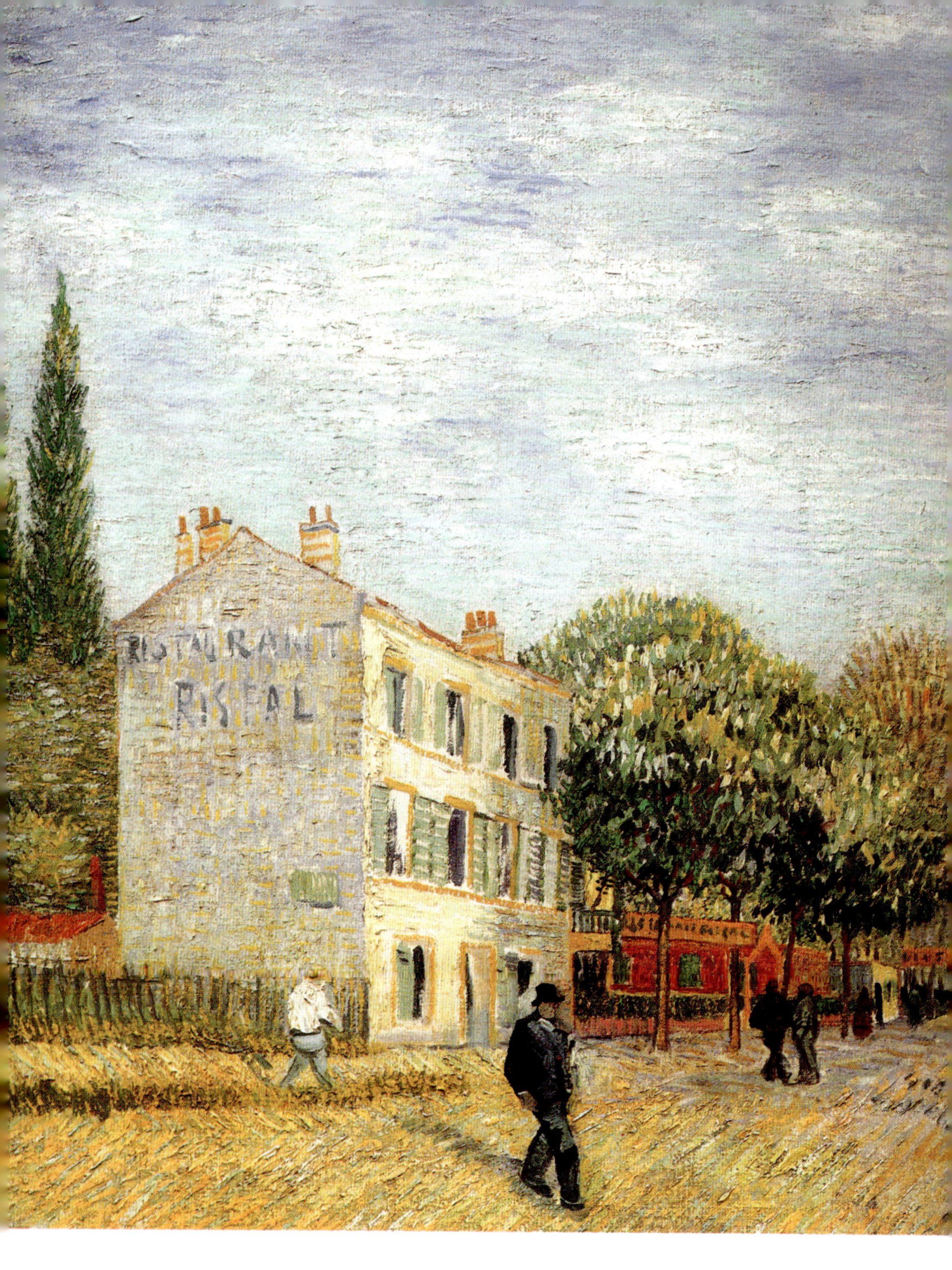
RESTAURANT
RISPAL

'And yet it's really beautiful in the city sometimes, don't you agree?'

While Vincent definitely felt 'more *at home* in the country' (490), from time to time he enjoyed city life. After all, in a city – and he lived in Brussels, The Hague, Antwerp and Paris during his artistic career – he could meet other artists, visit museums and art galleries, and tackle urban subject matter. When he arrived in Antwerp in November 1885, following a two-year stay with his parents in rural Brabant, he explained to Theo the pleasure he felt when exploring a large, dynamic city again: 'How much good it does me – much as I love the peasants and countryside – to observe a city again' (551).

As a true countryman, he remained fascinated by trees even when he was living in towns and cities. Before, woods and rural lanes had been the focus of his tree compositions, now – with urban streets and squares – he was more interested in the juxtaposition of the natural forms of the trees and the complex geometry of the buildings. Working on canvases in the country he could concentrate entirely on the natural qualities of the trees, whereas in his townscape views it was the contrast of the trees and their often mundane settings that led to intriguing compositions [34].

In addition, the trees that he encountered in towns and cities provided Vincent with a welcome reminder of the countryside, where everything, he felt, 'speaks more clearly, everything holds firm, everything explains itself' (841). Due to his peripatetic existence as an artist, Van Gogh lived in eleven places in ten years – five villages, two towns and four cities. This restlessness also illustrated the deep-rooted feelings of anxiety and uncertainty that had been in evidence much earlier in his life. In 1876, while working as an assistant curate in Isleworth near London, Vincent had written and delivered his famous sermon in English. Significantly, he had selected as his theme Psalm 119:19,

OPPOSITE
[34] *The Rispal Restaurant at Asnières*
Paris, Summer 1887
Van Gogh would often walk from central Paris to the suburb of Asnières accompanied by his closest friend, the painter and writer Émile Bernard (1868–1941), whose family resided there. The restaurant, nestling among the trees, was a well-known landmark. In the painting the red of the neighbouring buildings is intensified by the complementary green of the leaves, and over half of the composition is devoted to the sky; a device used to convey the openness of the suburban location.

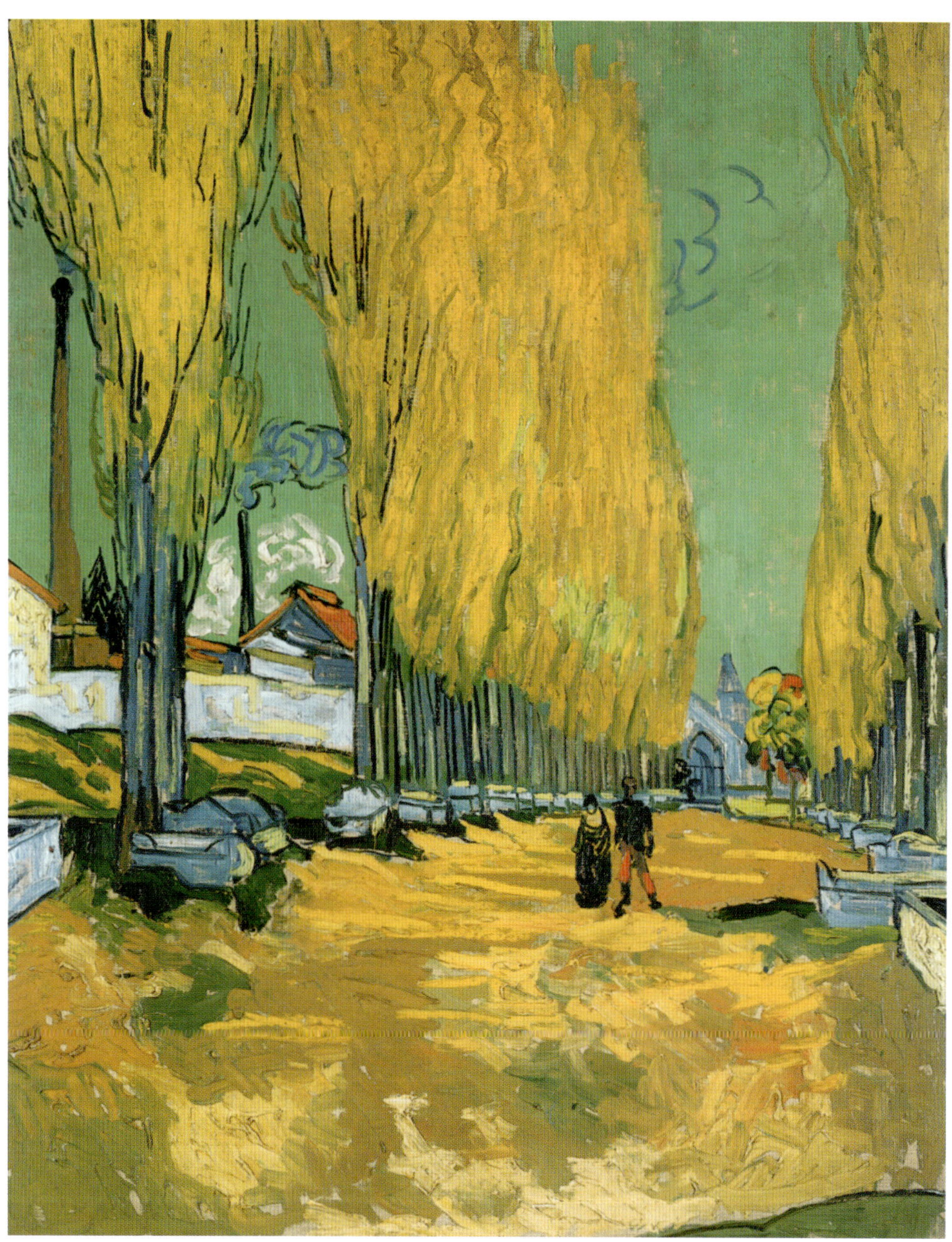

[35] *Les Alyscamps*
Arles, late October 1888
During his stay in Arles, Vincent once again tackled one of his favourite motifs – an avenue lined with elegant poplars. In this urban location, however, he juxtaposed the verticality of the trees with the tall chimney stacks of the adjoining factory complex.

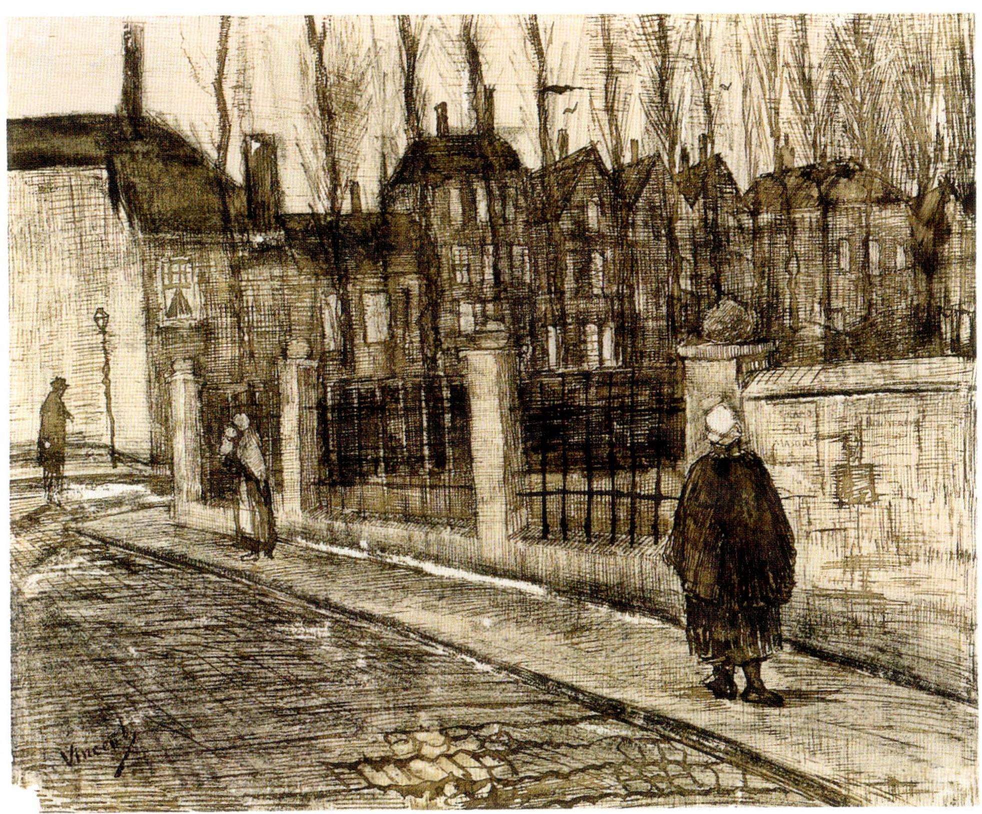

'I am a stranger on the earth'. For all his life he identified
with many of the sentiments expressed in the sermon, mainly
the view that, in essence, 'We are pilgrims on the earth and
strangers' (96). He never felt that he truly belonged anywhere
and became something of a misfit wherever he chose to settle,
but this perspective of the perpetual outsider heightened his
awareness of the distinctive qualities of each place. He saw
each subsequent townscape through the eyes of a perceptive
newcomer and with the mind of an artistic 'stranger'.

Although he never remained for more than two years in
any one place during his career, his output as an artist was
all the richer because of his ongoing quest for stimulating
new scenes to explore. In his drawings of village streets,
trees often appear as natural foils for the local architecture.
When living in towns, for example in Arles, where he stayed
between 21 February 1888 and 8 May 1889, he remained

[36] *The Paddemoes*
Pencil and ink on wove paper
The Hague, February–March 1882
Vincent was walking late at night
in The Hague when he encountered
this streetscape. He sketched the
basic composition in pencil, then
'set to work on it again the next
morning with the pen' (211). It was
on the basis of the quality of this
work that Vincent's uncle, the art
dealer Cornelis Marinus van Gogh
(1826–1908), referred to as 'Uncle
Cor' or C. M., commissioned his
nephew to prepare two series of
drawings depicting urban scenes.
This drawing, with its delicate
screen of leafless trees, was therefore
a major commercial breakthrough
for Vincent, especially considering
his early ambition to become an
illustrator and printmaker.

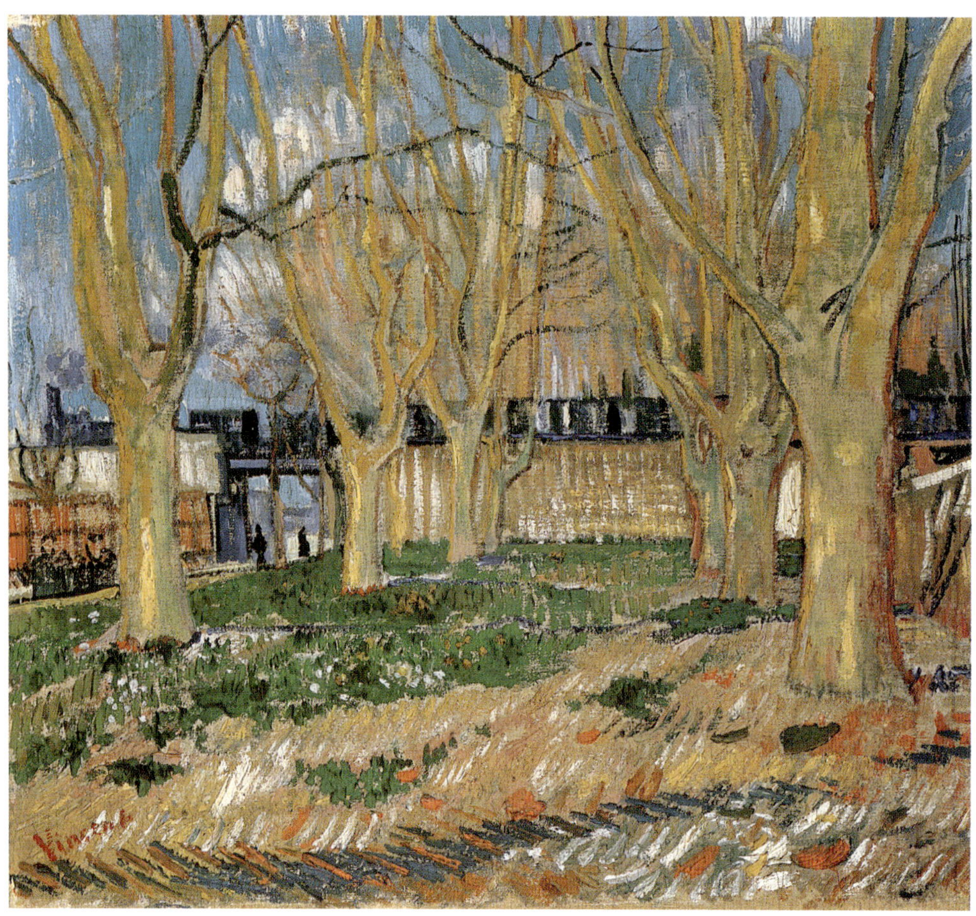

[37] *Avenue of Plane
Trees near Arles Station*
Arles, March 1888
In this unconventional composition,
an avenue of enormous plane trees
was set against the strong horizontal
band created by the railway line
and the train itself. The highlights
on the tree trunks and interlocking
branches suggest bright sunlight.

a countryman at heart but never shrank from painting trees
in conjunction with new urban elements such as bridges,
railways and factories [35]. Indeed, in his commitment
to the accurate depiction of townscapes, Vincent again
echoed Dutch traditions of visual art, especially of the
seventeenth century.

Just as his rambles in the countryside provided him with
engrossing subject matter, so Vincent's long walks in cities
and towns also led him to discover 'nice scenes' (361). These
were often places where trees were dominant features in the
man-made environment, and could play a major part in his
compositions [36]. While living in The Hague, he was often
accompanied on his city walks by the Dutch painter George
Hendrik Breitner (1857–1923), who, like Vincent, was interested
in using street life as subject matter in his work. Vincent
was dismayed by the attitude of most other painters based
in The Hague, who found the city unattractive and preferred

[38] *A Guinguette*
Pencil, pen and brush in black
ink and white chalk on laid paper
(originally blue-grey)
Paris, February–March 1887
This drawing depicts a small Paris
café for workers – known as a
guinguette – located in Montmartre,
with an open-air terrace and
adjacent dance hall. The outlines
of the skeletal tree branches
add visual interest to the bleak
atmosphere of the sparsely
populated terrace. The drawing
hints at the loneliness Vincent
experienced in Paris during the
winter months.

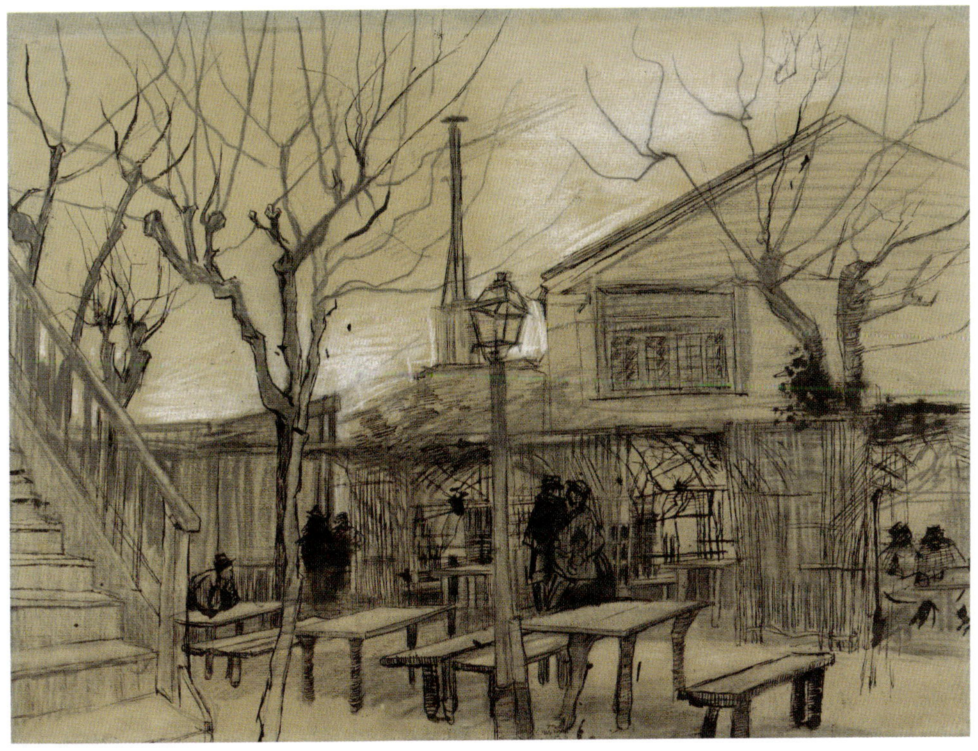

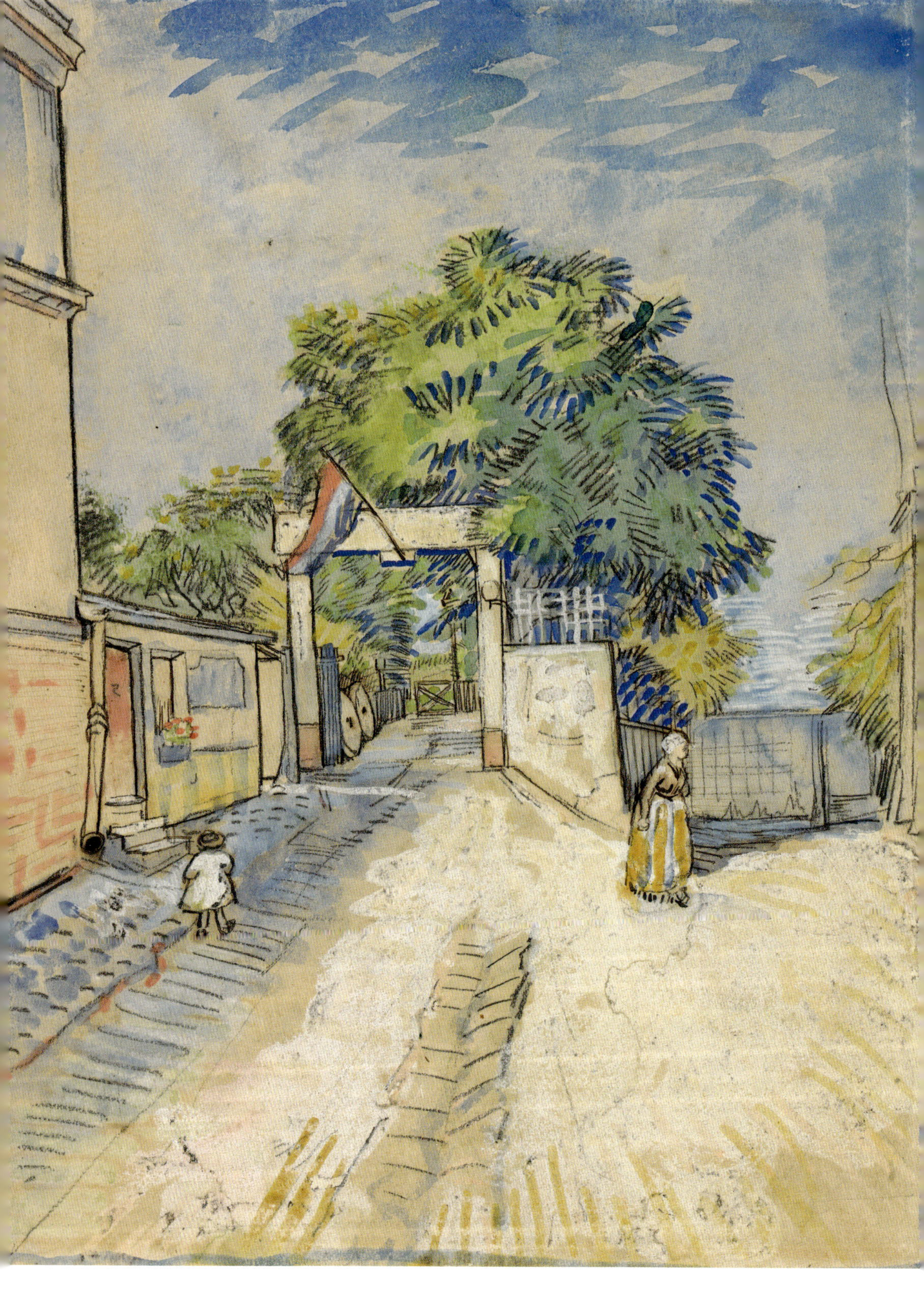

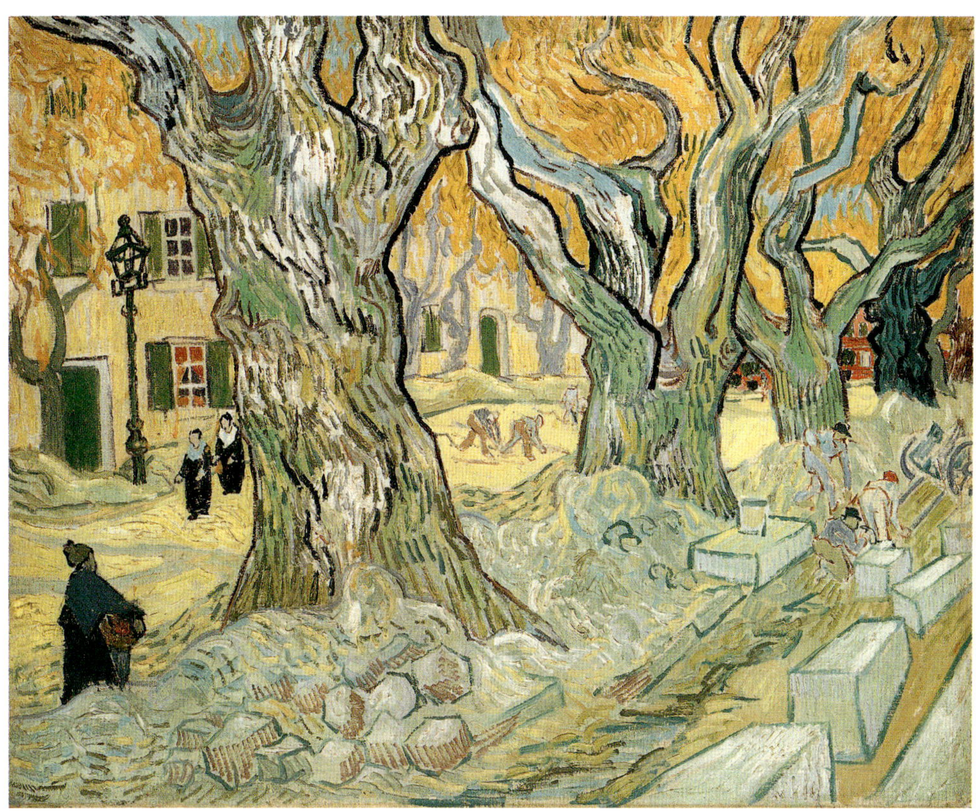

OPPOSITE
[39] *The Entrance to the
Moulin de la Galette*
Transparent and opaque watercolour,
pen ink and graphite on wove paper
Paris, Spring 1887
Vincent's expertise with the
watercolour medium is evident
in this painting, depicting the gate
to the Moulin de la Galette, a popular
entertainment area. The trees, newly
in leaf, dominate the composition
and soften the architectural forms.

ABOVE
[40] *The Road Menders*
Saint-Rémy, November 1889
Writing to his friend, the painter
Paul Gauguin (1848–1903),
Vincent concluded that seemingly
unprepossessing places in Provence
revealed their visual interest only
after a considerable period of
study: 'It's in the long term that
the poetry down here soaks in' (706).
In this painting, the visual poetry
stems from differences of scale:
Vincent was particularly interested
in emphasizing the monumental
scale of the trees in relation to the
diminutive workers and passers-by.

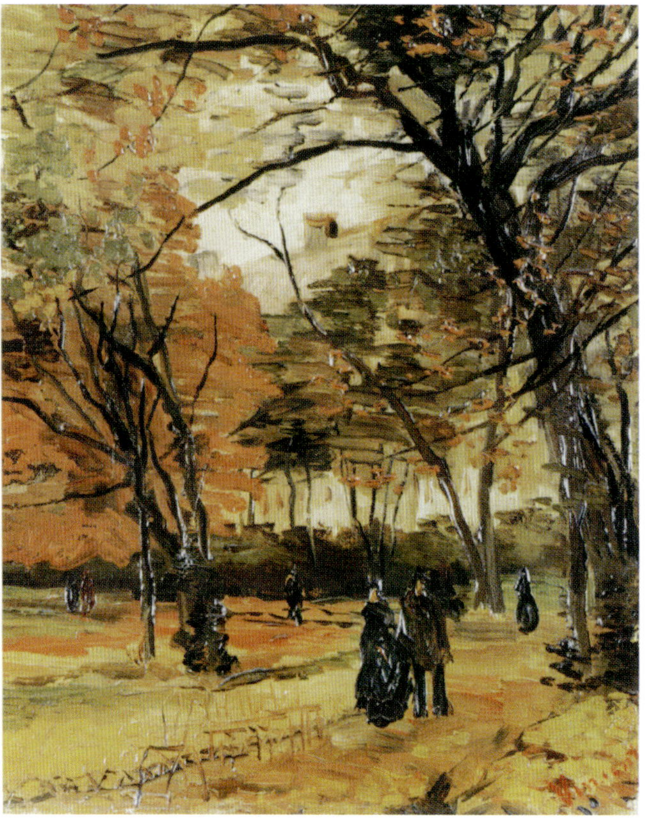

[41] *Scene in a Park*
Paris, Autumn 1886
For Vincent, the Parisian parks
were wooded arenas for experiments
with figure composition. It was
the juxtaposition of the trees
and the strolling figures that
captured his imagination.

to concentrate on landscape painting. Neither Breitner nor
Van Gogh perceived the city as ugly, the latter explaining:
'The Hague is beautiful – there's enormous diversity' (325).

Trees growing in streets, squares, parks and gardens
were part of the visual diversity of the urban vistas that
Vincent found so attractive in the places where he lived.
But – not wishing to produce sentimental images – he avoided
conventionally picturesque townscapes as motifs, preferring
instead locations that were evocative of everyday life [37].
His extensive reading of nineteenth-century novels also made
him particularly receptive to urban scenes where recent social
and economic changes were evident, for example where the
impact of industrialization and the railways could be seen:
'Books and reality and art', wrote Vincent, 'are the same kind
of thing for me' (312).

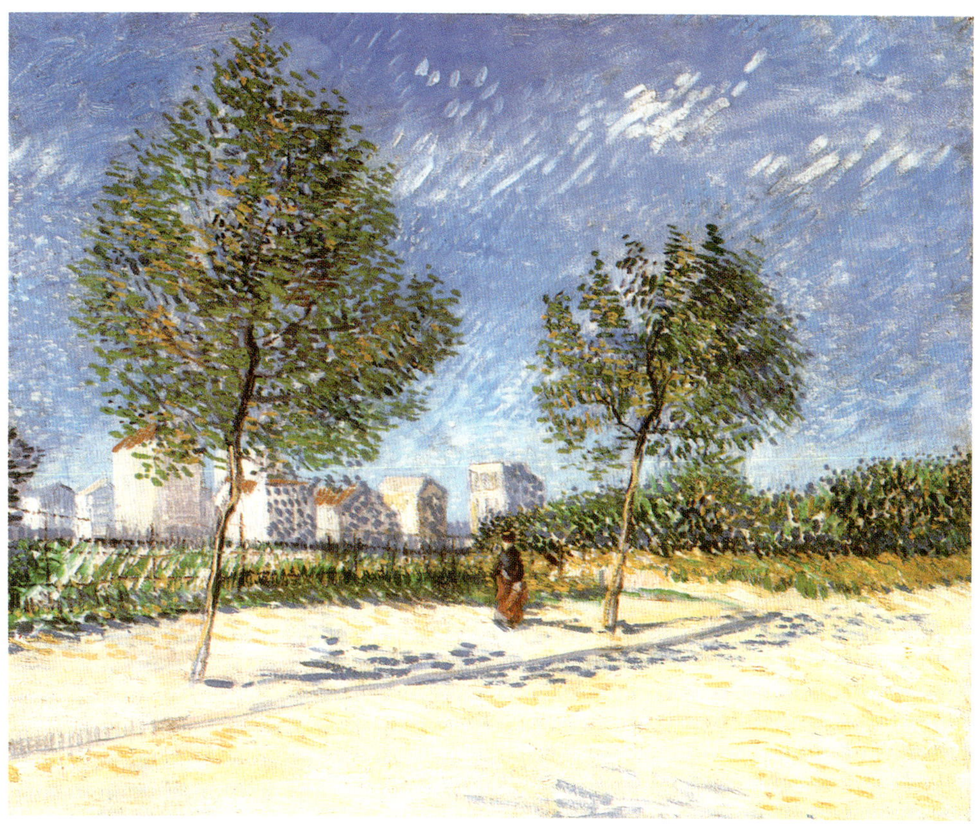

[42] *On the Outskirts of Paris*
Paris, Spring 1887
With its shimmering trees, large expanse of blue sky and dominant sun-drenched foreground, this canvas illustrates Vincent's new commitment to bright colours. In this he was influenced by the Impressionist paintings he had seen in Paris. Writing to his youngest sister, Wil (Willemien van Gogh, 1862–1941), he stated that 'what people want in art nowadays has to be very lively, with strong colour, very intense' (574).

Van Gogh's aphorism 'Poetry surrounds us everywhere' (330) summarizes his amalgam of literary appreciation, social realism and aesthetic perception. Taking his cue from novelists and poets of his generation, he decided that in his own work, quite ordinary and untidy places could form the basis of harmonious compositions. When living in Paris from 1886 to 1888, he sometimes selected rather shabby locations or working-class scenes as the basis for his drawings and paintings. However, even in winter, trees often transformed the character of these sites [38]. When he was living in Montmartre, he noticed that clusters of trees in full leaf could alter nondescript buildings completely [39]. Even when he selected municipal construction works for his subject matter, such as the roadworks in Saint-Rémy-de-Provence, it was the powerful imagery of trees that dominated his portrayal of these contemporary settings [40].

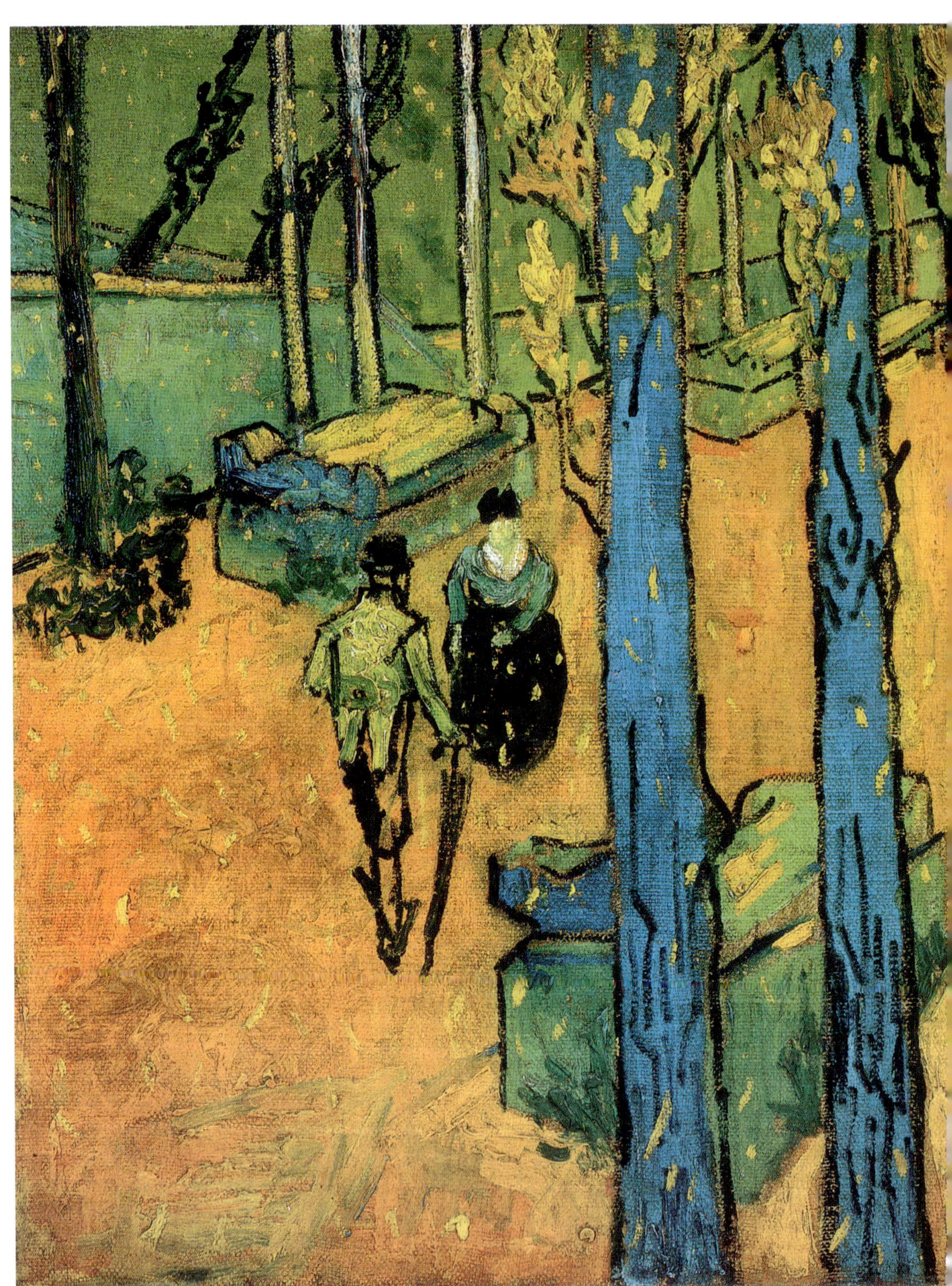

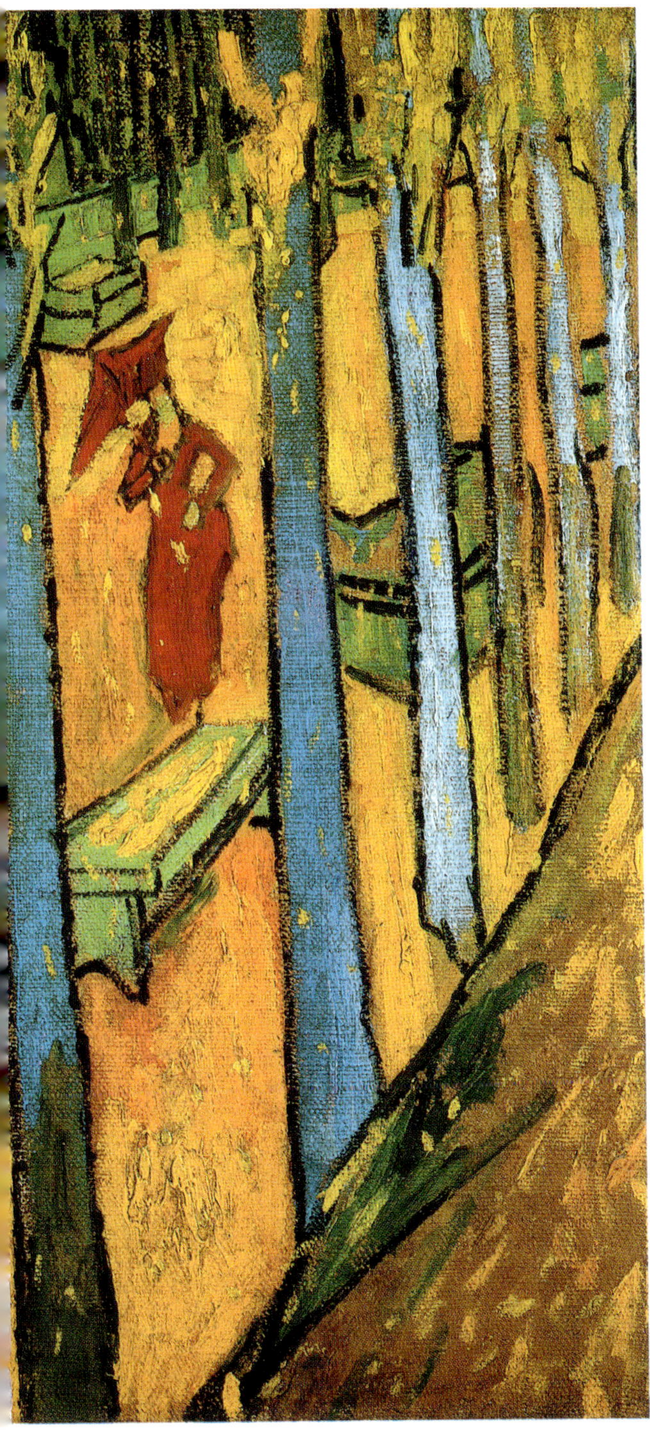

[43] *Les Alyscamps,
Falling Autumn Leaves*
Arles, November 1888
Showing the influence of stylized
compositions by his friends Bernard
and Gauguin, Van Gogh's painting
of this historic route, bordered by
Roman sarcophagi, also reveals
his great admiration for Japanese
prints. The bright colours, dark
outlining of forms and dramatic
foreshortening all point to this
influence. Vincent likened the
trees to 'pillars' and noted that
the leaves were 'still falling,
like snowflakes' (717).

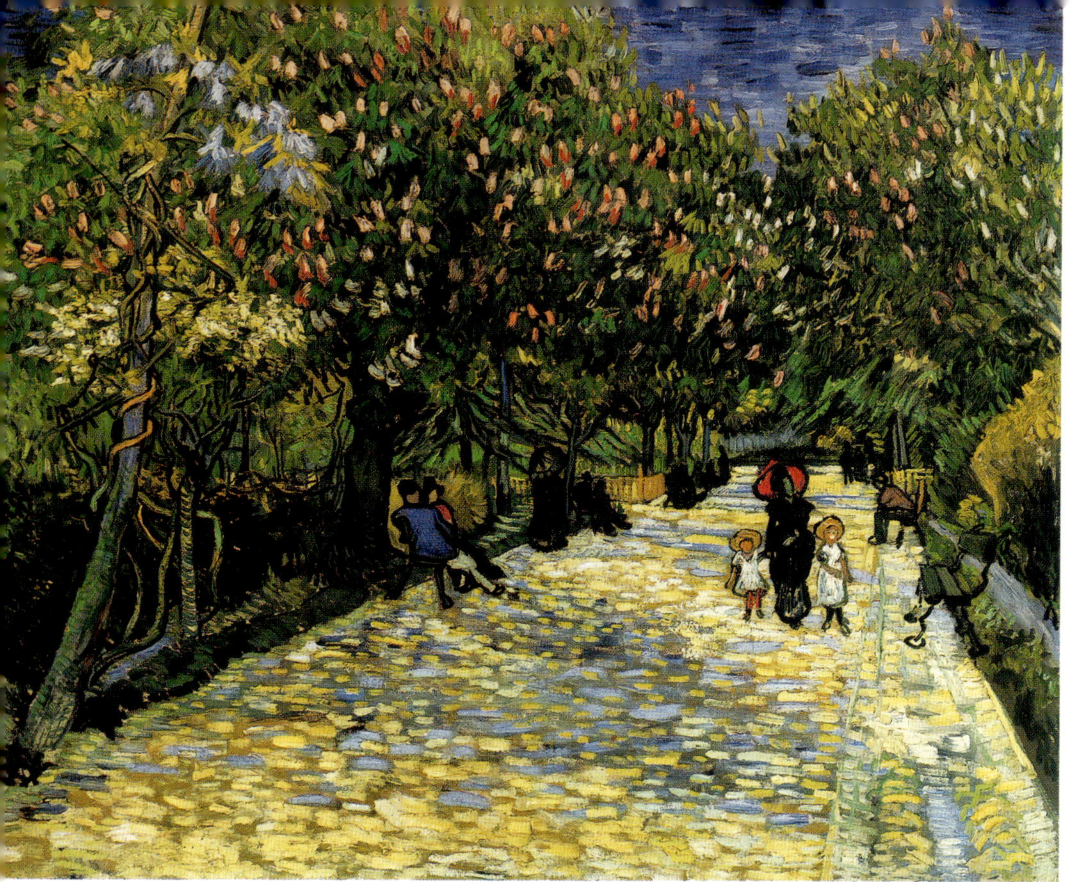

However, it required an artist of Van Gogh's talent to perceive the poetry in such humdrum places, and to convince the viewer that, indeed, it 'surrounds us everywhere' (330).

It was not just in the working-class districts of Paris that Vincent found trees to draw and paint. Fashionable parks, such as the Bois de Boulogne, gave him the opportunity to create images with a visual interplay between trees, well-dressed figures and civic architecture [41]. For Vincent, the parks seemed to bring elements of the countryside to the heart of a crowded city. During his long walks, he also explored the new suburbs of Paris, with their recently constructed apartment blocks and wide roads planted with lines of young trees. As can be seen in one of his paintings, the delicacy and fragility of the saplings was in stark contrast with the geometric severity of the buildings and the road network [42]. To Vincent, these slender trees seemed like symbols of nature in a bare, man-made world.

While living in Arles, Vincent was attracted by urban subject matter as well as the rural hinterland. In his paintings of the streets, he often chose to make trees the main focus of his compositions. One historic avenue in particular, Les Alyscamps, captured his imagination with its regular planting of tall poplars, resulting in images of great originality [43]. The public gardens near the Place Lamartine boasted a large number of tree species and, as subject matter, these proved irresistible to an artist who at the beginning of his career had painted woods and gardens in the Netherlands. Located very close to Vincent's studio and apartment ('The Yellow House'), these secluded gardens inspired him to create some of his most richly patterned paintings and drawings [44] [45].

From 21 May 1890 until his death on 29 July 1890, Van Gogh lived in the large village of Auvers-sur-Oise near Paris. The village was quiet and rural, and retained some of its historic thatched houses. In the main streets, the small open spaces

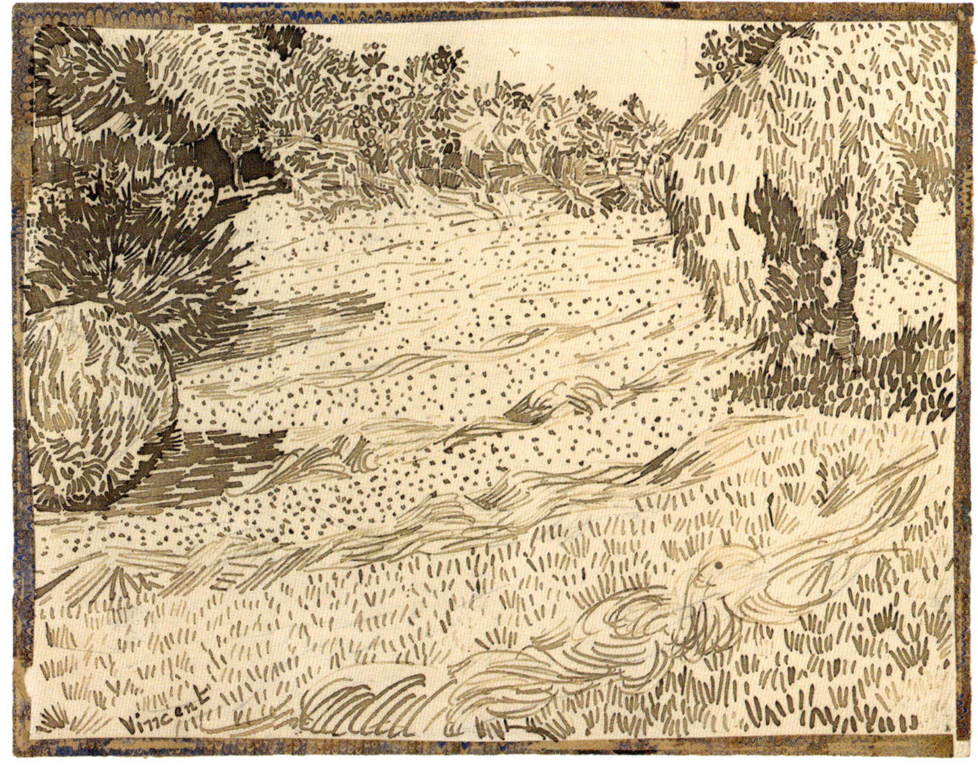

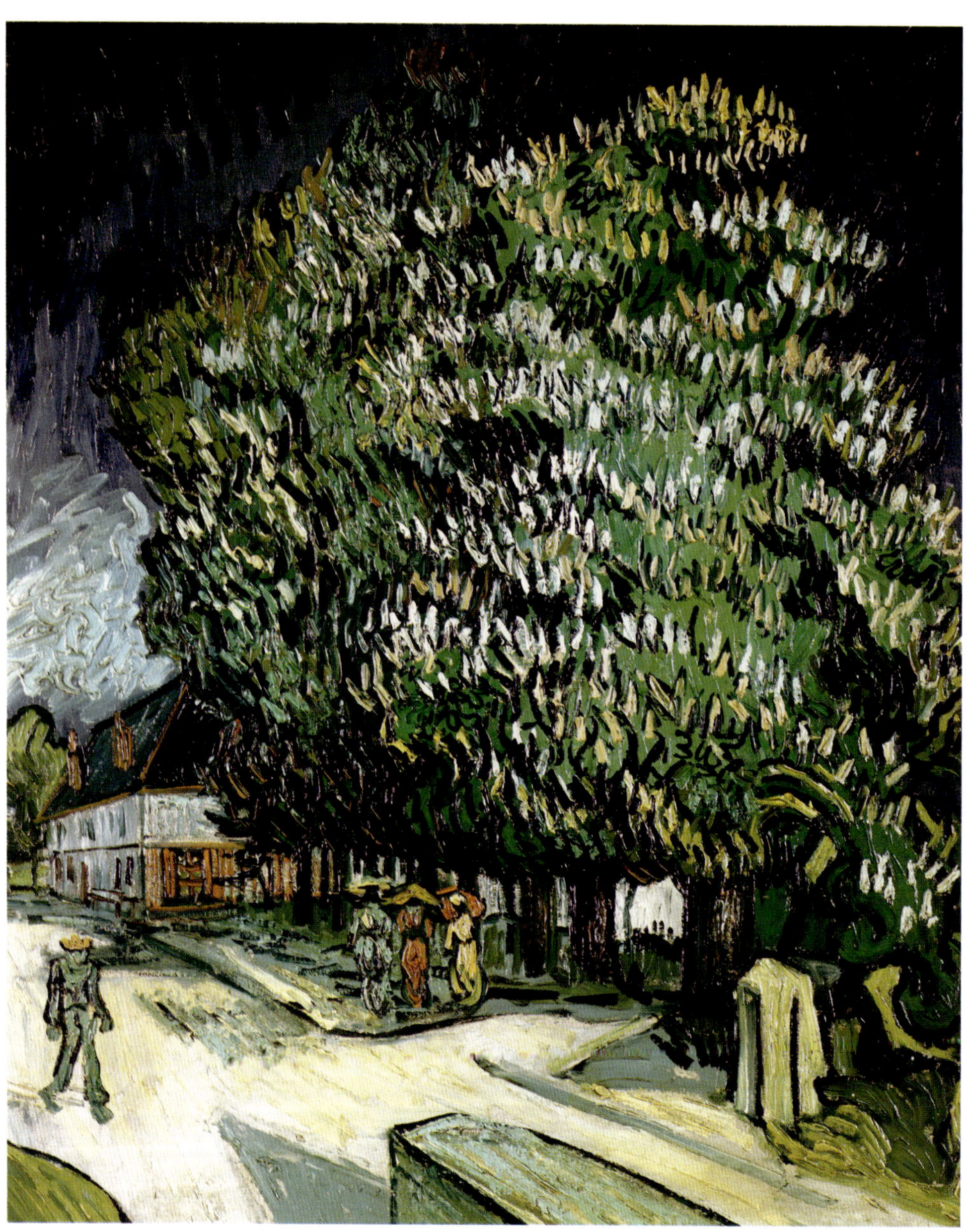

[46] *Chestnut Trees in Blossom*
Auvers-sur-Oise, May 1890
The enormous scale of the chestnut trees in this canvas is accentuated by the tiny figures walking in the street. The exuberance of the blossom and leaves is shown in a complex pattern of brushstrokes and graphic marks. The bright sunshine bathing the street contrasts with the dark, rain-threatening sky.

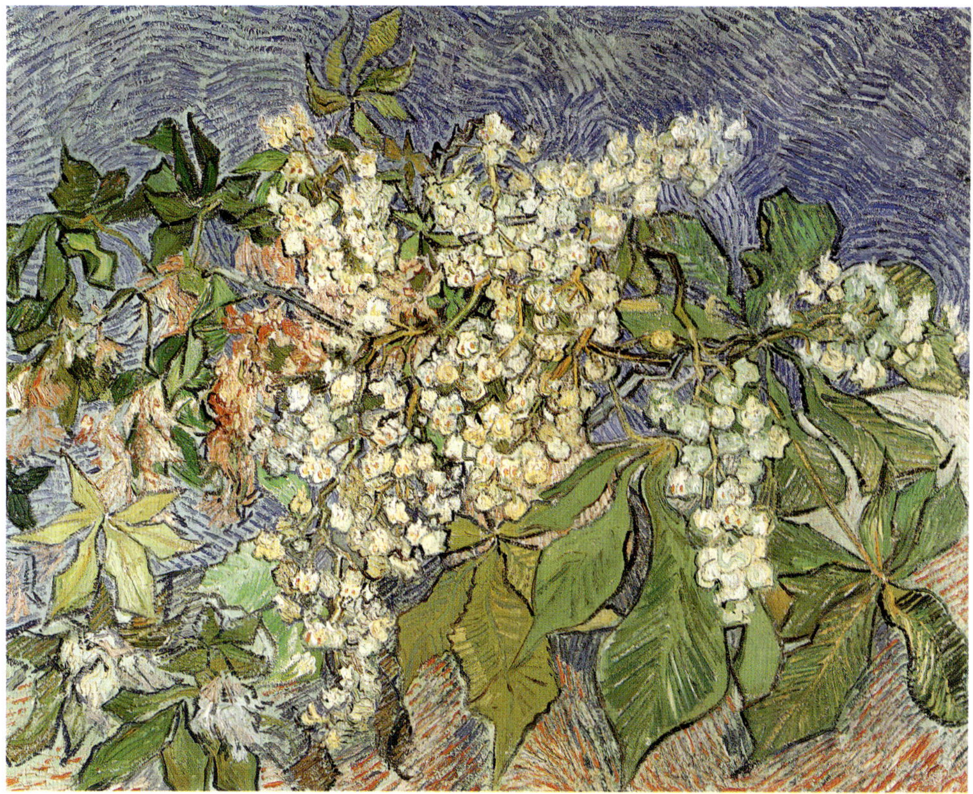

and villa gardens he painted the blossoming chestnut trees that seemed to engulf the small buildings with their explosions of leaves and flowers [46]. In a related painting, conceived as a close-up study of tree branches, Vincent successfully conveyed the intricate nature of the flowering chestnut tree [47].

By his own admission, Vincent found it difficult to adapt to life in towns and cities, but trees growing in these urban places supplied him with compelling motifs and lifted his spirits when he felt overwhelmed by the noise and crowds. They acted as a natural antithesis to the inert character of the buildings within the townscape and reminded Vincent of the countryside, where he always felt he should be living.

[47] *Blossoming Chestnut Branches*
Auvers-sur-Oise, May 1890
Vincent studied the blossoming chestnut branches with great intensity. The use of elaborate patterning for all aspects of the composition resulted in an image that possesses the characteristics of a richly embroidered fabric.

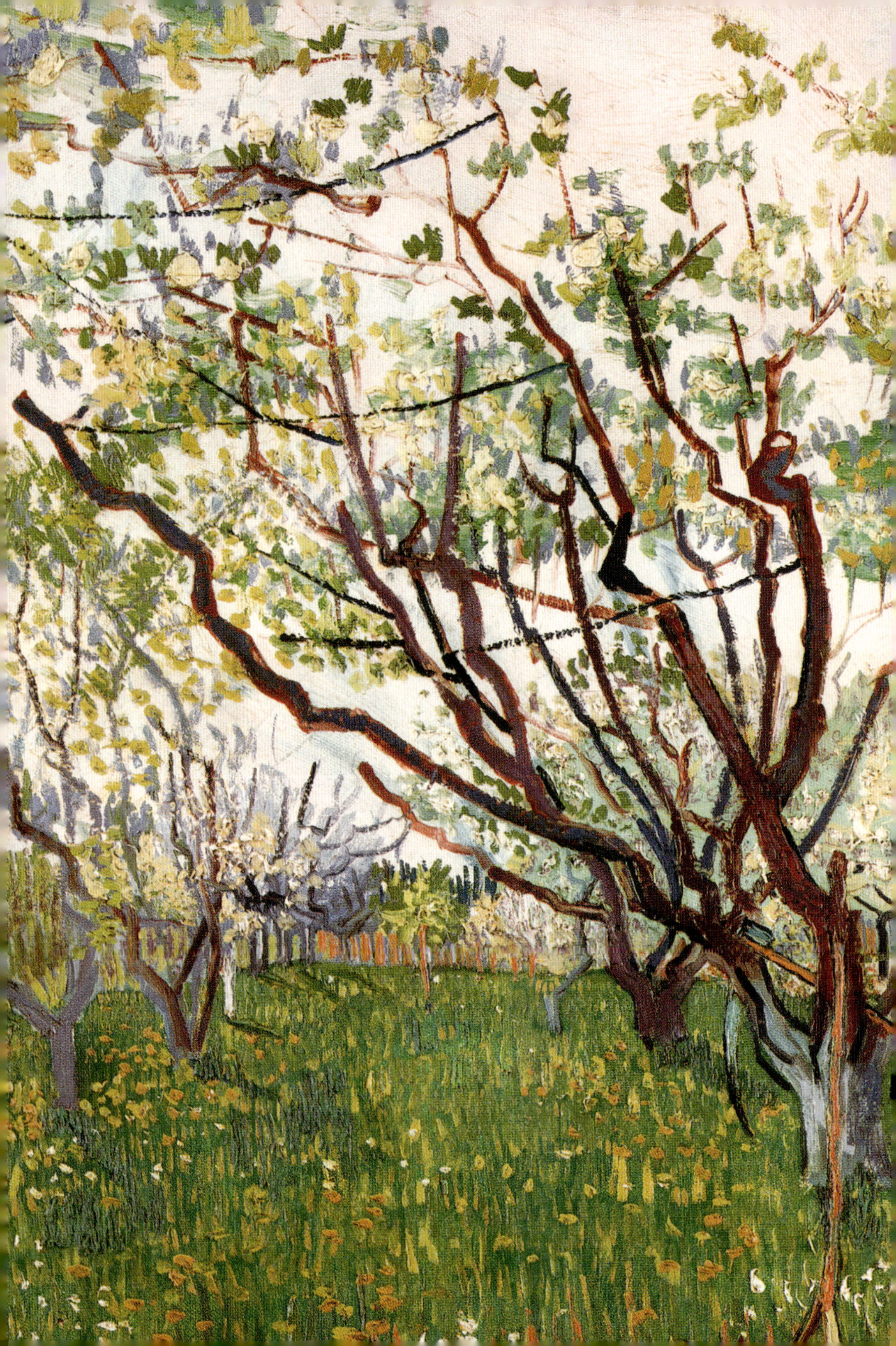

CHAPTER 4

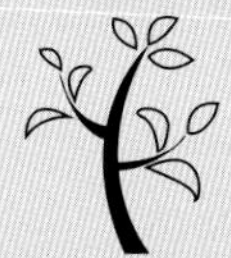

Vincent's Orchards

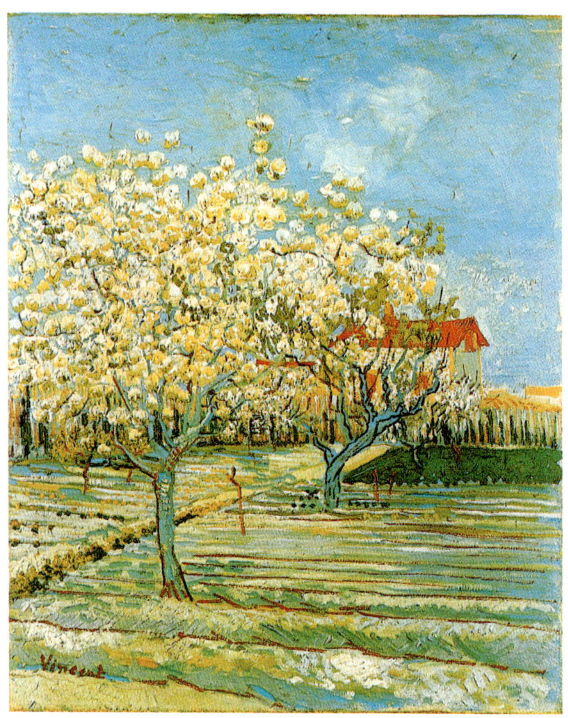

LEFT
[48] *Orchard with
Pear Trees in Blossom*
Arles, May 1888
In a letter to Bernard, Van Gogh
described this orchard painting as
'quite simple in composition' (599).
He viewed this as a positive feature,
however, and gave the canvas to
Theo on his birthday. Vincent
summed up the painting's nature
and the techniques he had used in
its creation with his characteristic
enthusiasm: 'It's entirely bright
and done entirely in one go, a riot
of impasto barely tinged with
yellow and lilac in the first white
clump' (600).

RIGHT
[49] *Orchard in Blossom
(Apricot Trees)*
Arles, April 1888
By juxtaposing the fruit orchard
with the factory chimney in the
background, Van Gogh brought
together ancient and modern
aspects of Provençal life in this
canvas. He hoped that some of
his orchard paintings would be
displayed as triptychs, and this
work was probably intended
as a left panel.

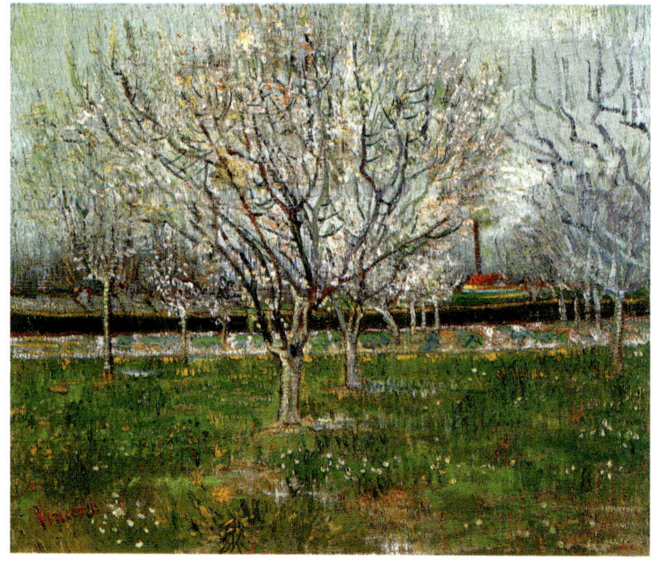

'This rage to paint orchards won't last forever.'

In late February 1888, Vincent informed his sister Wil that he had left northern France and had 'gone somewhat further to the south' (579). He had settled in the large Provençal town of Arles, near the mouth of the river Rhône. The warm climate of the south of France, he hoped, would improve his constitution. Moreover, with its promise of clear skies and bright colours, he speculated that it could perhaps help him to produce livelier canvases: 'Nowadays people are demanding colour contrasts and highly intense and variegated colours in paintings rather than a subdued grey colour' (579). His speculation was prophetic in terms of the famous work he was to create in and around Arles and Saint-Rémy between February 1888 and May 1890, especially his orchard paintings [48].

Initially, however, his hopes for southern warmth were dashed. When he arrived in Arles on 21 February 1888 it was snowing; undaunted, he produced attractive snow scenes of the neighbouring countryside. By 16 March the weather had started to improve, accompanied by the spectacular blossoming of the almond trees in the orchards around Arles: 'The weather's changeable, often windy and cloudy skies – but the almond trees are starting to blossom everywhere' (585). Over the next month, he was to complete fourteen large canvases of orchards in blossom, not only almond trees, but also apple, peach, plum, pear and apricot [49].

In 1882, while living in the Netherlands, he had experimented with orchards as subject matter, inspired perhaps by similar paintings by two of his favourite painters, Charles-François Daubigny (1817–1878) and Jean-François Millet (1814–1875). Later, in Antwerp, he encountered the distinctive features of Japanese blockprints, many of which featured blossoming trees. In 1887, when living in Paris, Van Gogh even made a free interpretation of a print showing a plum tree in blossom.

Cypresses were planted around fruit
orchards to give maximum shelter
from the mistral. This painting,
which Van Gogh initially thought
to be 'too harsh' (615), also shows
the cane fencing that provided
added protection from the winds.

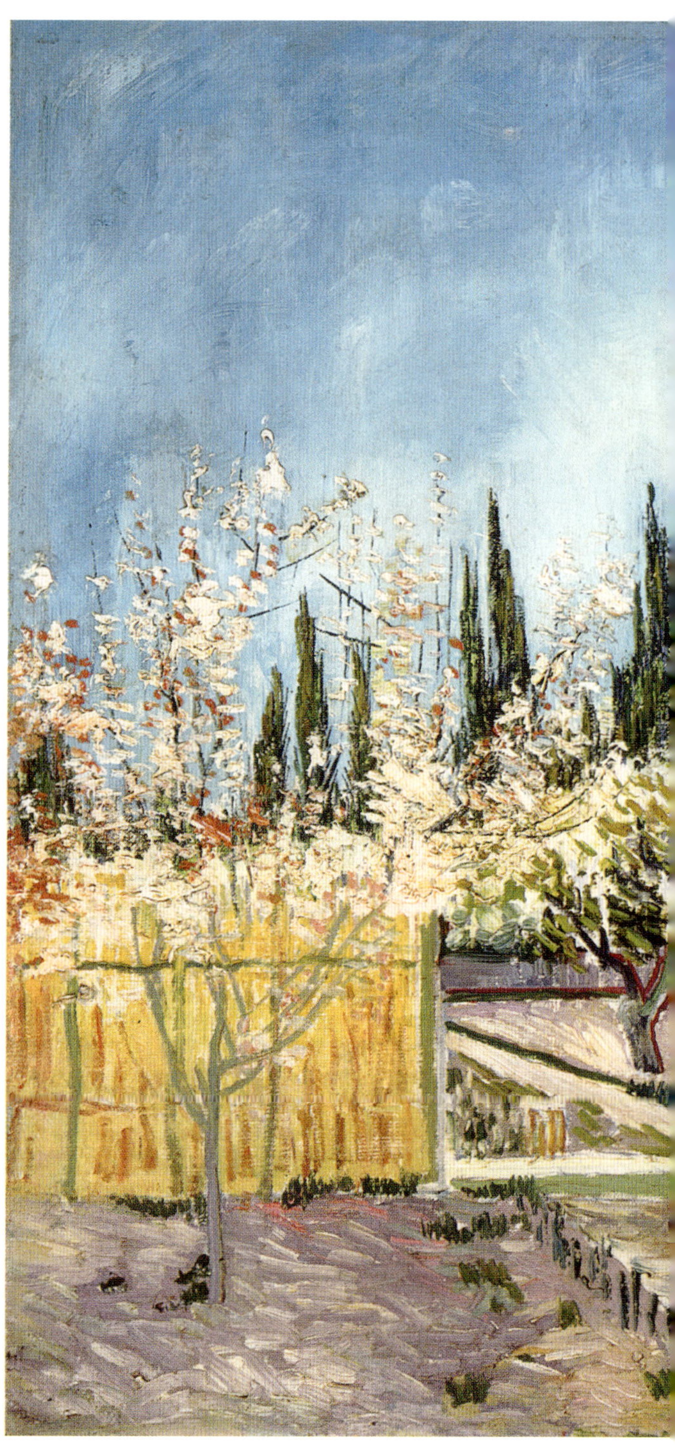

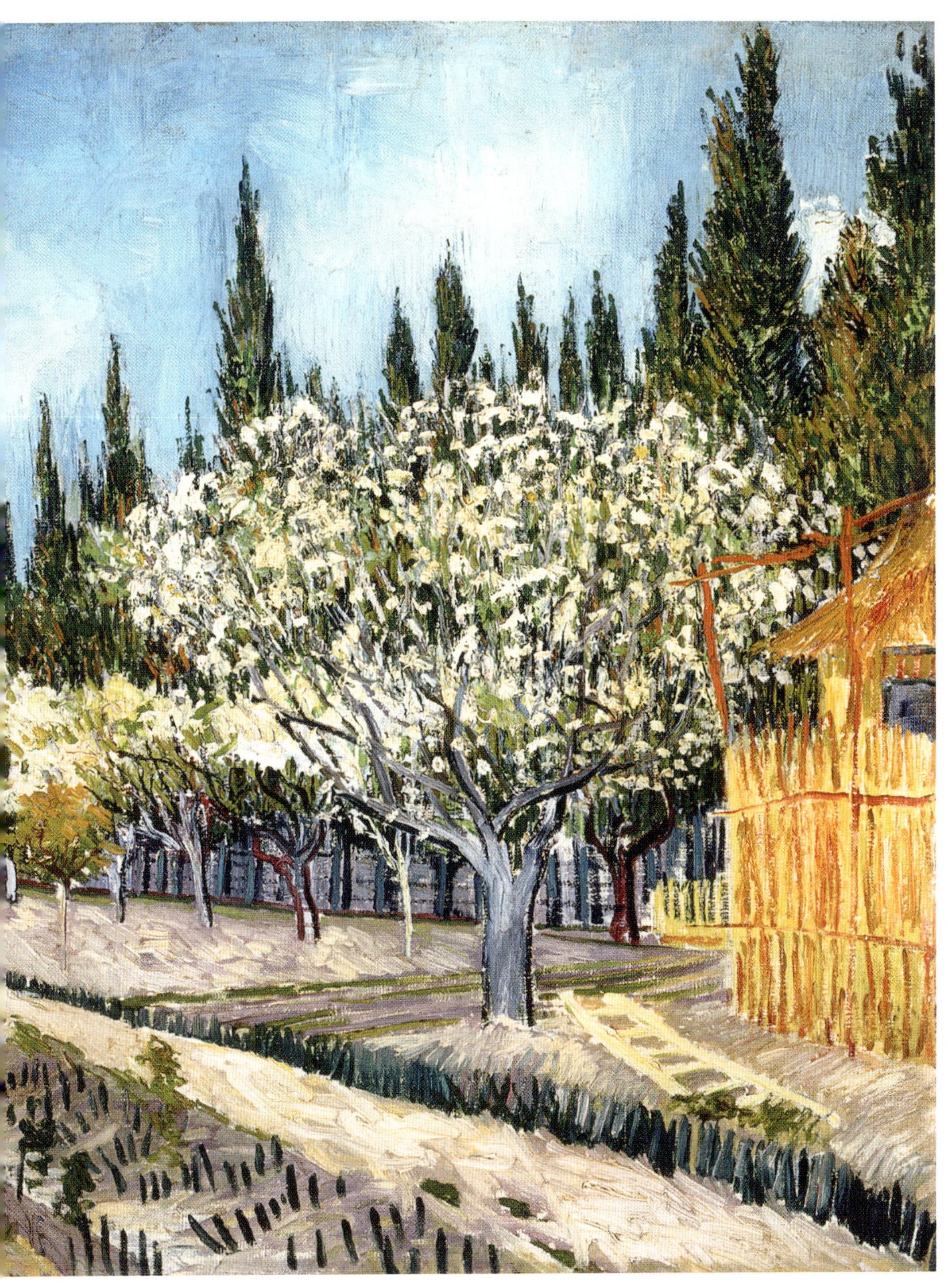

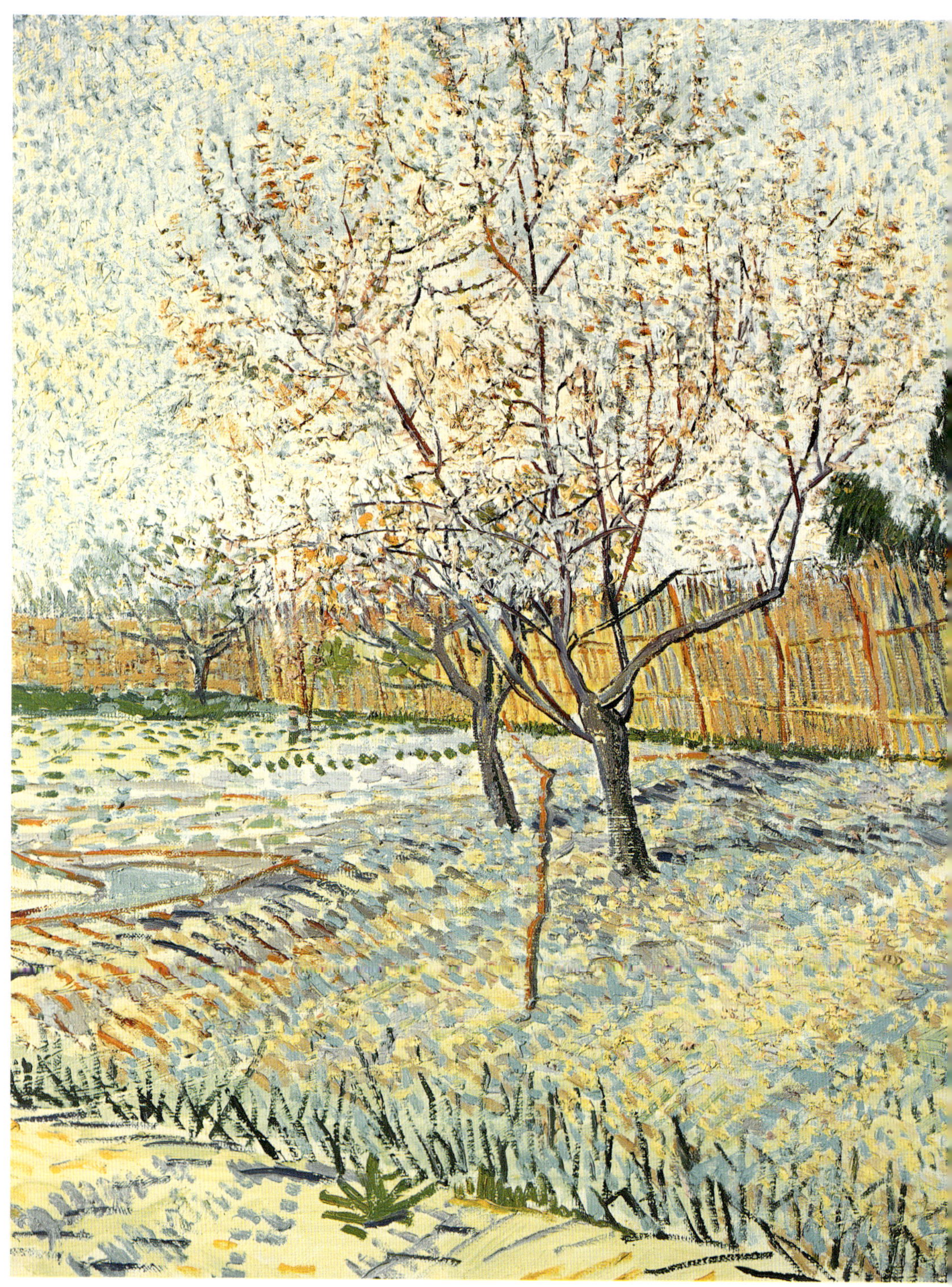

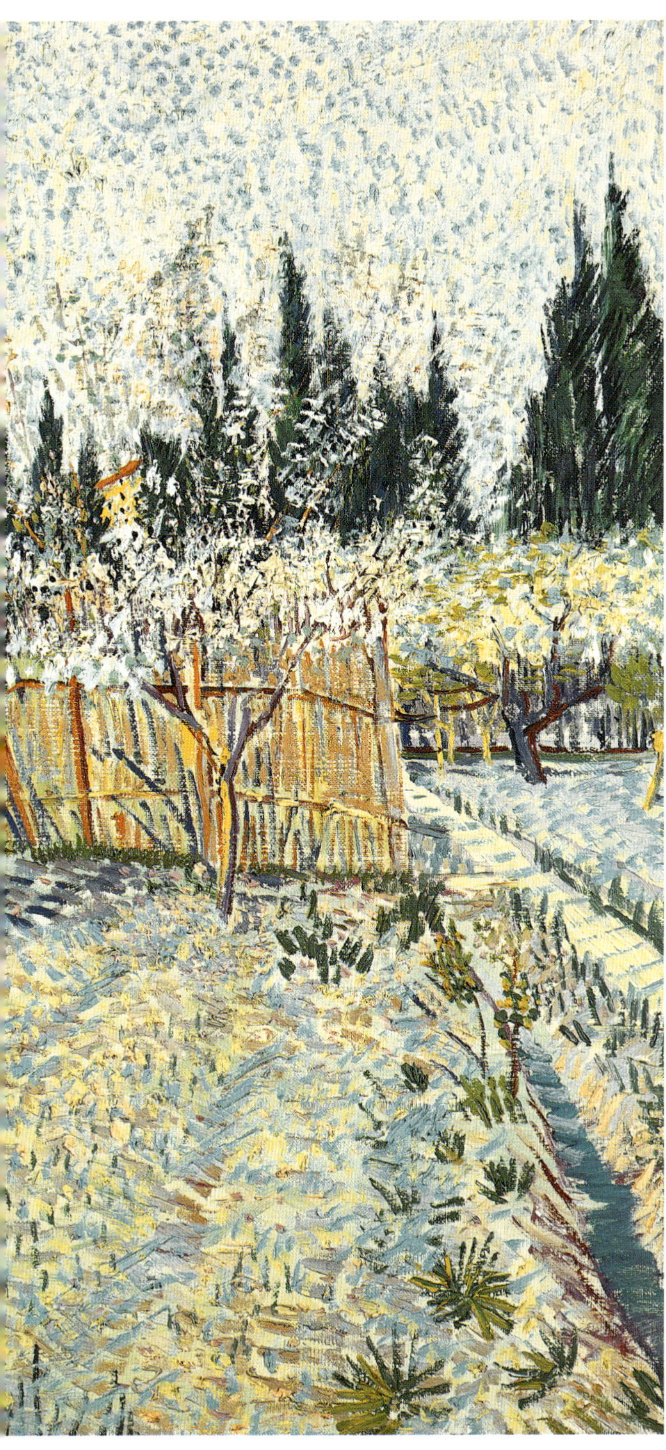

[51] *Orchard with Peach Blossom*
Arles, April 1888
This experiment in the Pointillist technique, which was pioneered by Georges Seurat (1859–1891) and Paul Signac (1863–1935), shows the typical small touches of pigment, used here to convey the brightness of a spring day in a peach orchard. Vincent's stippling is much 'freer' than that of the Pointillists and achieves a shimmering effect.

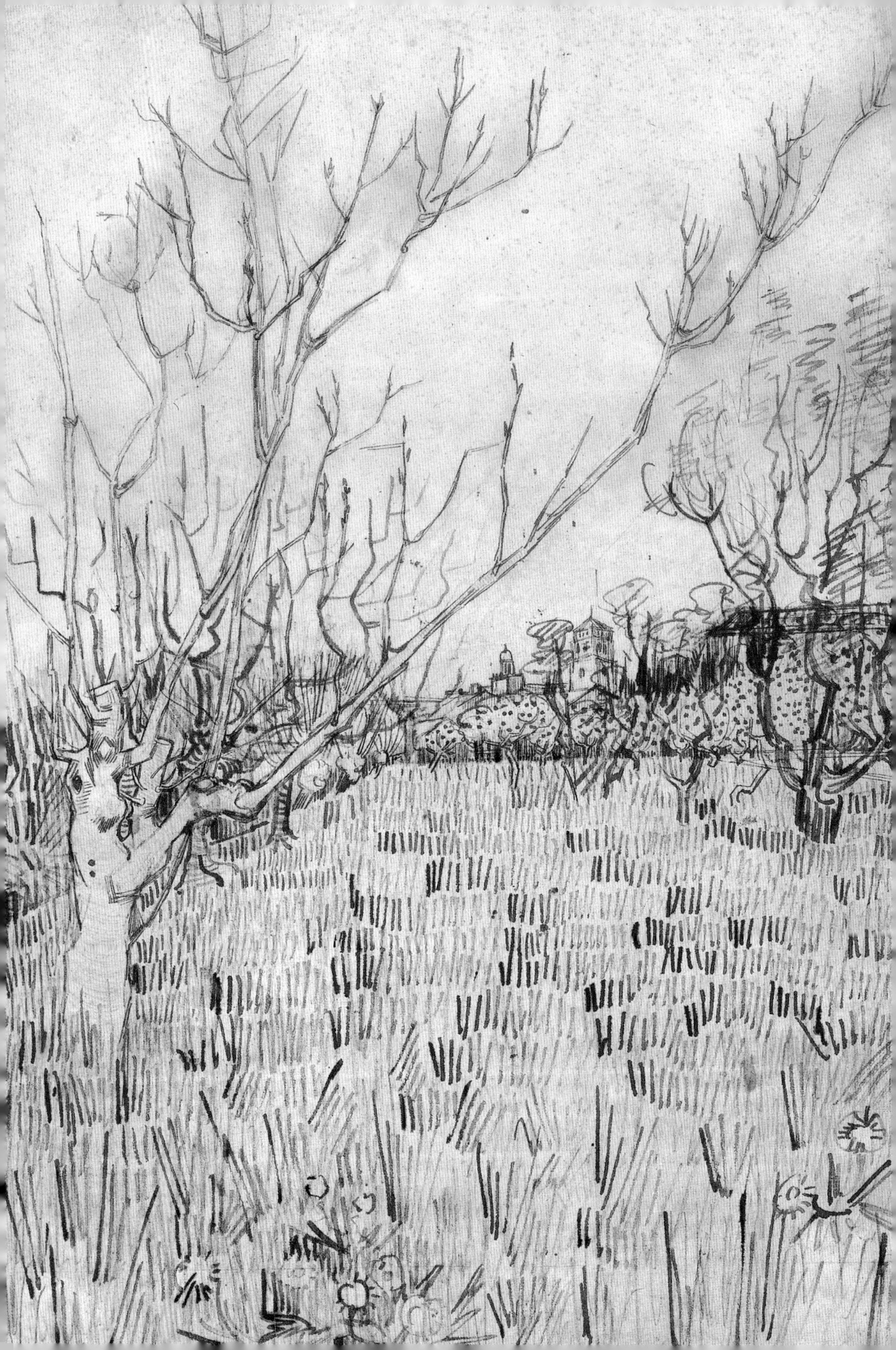

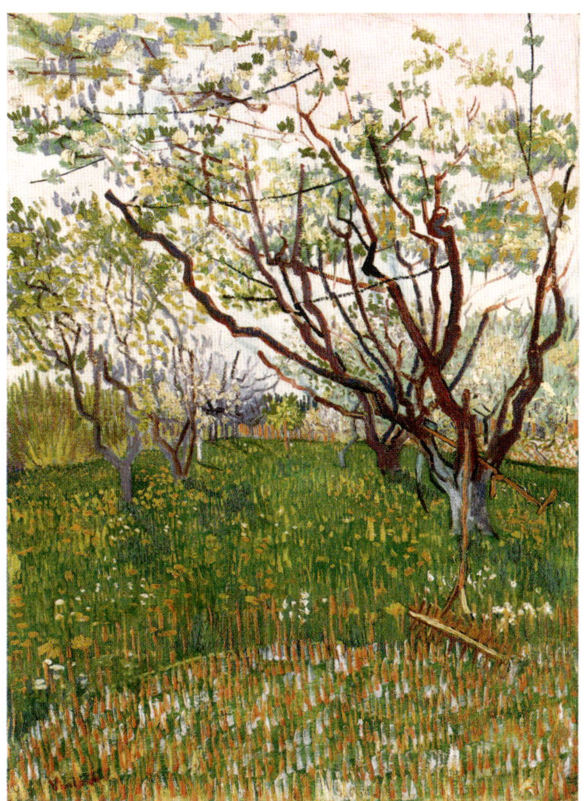

LEFT

[53] *Flowering Orchard*
Arles, April–May 1888
Many of Van Gogh's paintings
of orchards display a meticulous
attention to detail in terms of
composition, colour harmony
and draughtsmanship. Works
like this one provided him with
a sense of redemption: 'The uglier,
older, meaner, iller, poorer I get,
the more I wish to take my revenge
by doing brilliant colour, well
arranged, resplendent' (678).

This painting included, in the background, an orchard of the
kind he was to paint in the south of France. It was not only art
that inspired his interest in blossoming orchards as potential
subject matter, but also his own impressions and feelings.
Blossoms, he believed, were 'among the tenderest and most
pure things under the sun' (408). Although he was aware that
the orchard motif was not original and could easily result in
paintings that were mere clichés, he hoped that his southern
location would transform the subject. His interpretations
of the theme, he suggested, would be quite different because
of the Provençal landscape, which was 'undoubtedly much
richer and more colourful' (590) [50].

Vincent was subject to mood swings all his life, frequently
experiencing periods of depression, followed by sudden
bouts of manic enthusiasm. It is significant that one of his
favourite biblical quotations was from 2 Corinthians 6:10:

OPPOSITE

[52] *Orchard with Arles
in the Background*
Pencil, quill and reed pen with
violet and black ink on laid paper
Arles, late March–early April 1888
The secluded orchards around Arles
provided Vincent with his own
'outdoor studios'. In this drawing,
a large fruit tree that is not yet in
bloom dominates the foreground;
on the horizon, the towers of the
Church of Saint Trophime and the
town hall of Arles can be glimpsed.
The networks of short, vertical lines
cleverly convey the texture of grass.

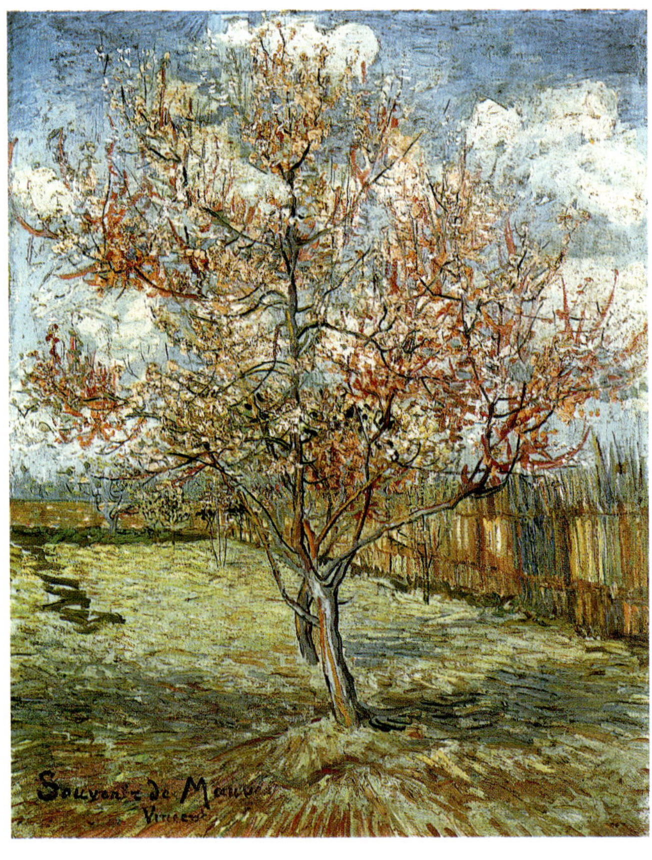

'sorrowful, yet always rejoicing' (89). Not solely reflecting his own disposition, the phrase also seems to underline his belief that while the human condition was essentially tragic, moments of rapture could be experienced and valued, especially by the artist. In the paintings of orchards in blossom, Vincent showed his extreme delight in what he perceived as joyful places. This series of images exemplified his belief that painting should celebrate the finest qualities of nature, thereby promoting well-being. Writing to Wil he summed up this optimistic view regarding the power of painting: 'My dear sister, I believe that at present we must paint nature's rich and magnificent aspects; we need good cheer and happiness, hope and love' (678). From his letters, we know that these were the very attributes Vincent sought to evoke in his paintings of flowering orchards [51].

Although the orchards were located near the built-up
areas of Arles, they were quiet, secluded places, especially
at blossom-time when there were few workers present.
Furthermore, due to the shelter provided by the cane fences,
the orchards were ideal sites for Vincent to work outdoors [52].
On windy days, however, when the mistral was blowing, he
had to improvise: 'I have a lot of trouble painting because of
the wind, but I fix my easel to pegs stuck in the ground and
work anyway, it's too beautiful' (591).

The orchards were in blossom for only a short period
of time, and Vincent made use of his abundant energy and
extraordinary technique to complete this series of works.
Despite the project, which he hoped to continue the following
spring, putting a strain on his nerves, he was determined
to capture the cheerful atmosphere he perceived in the
orchards: 'I'm in a fury of work as the trees are in blossom and
I wanted to do a Provence orchard of tremendous gaiety' (592).

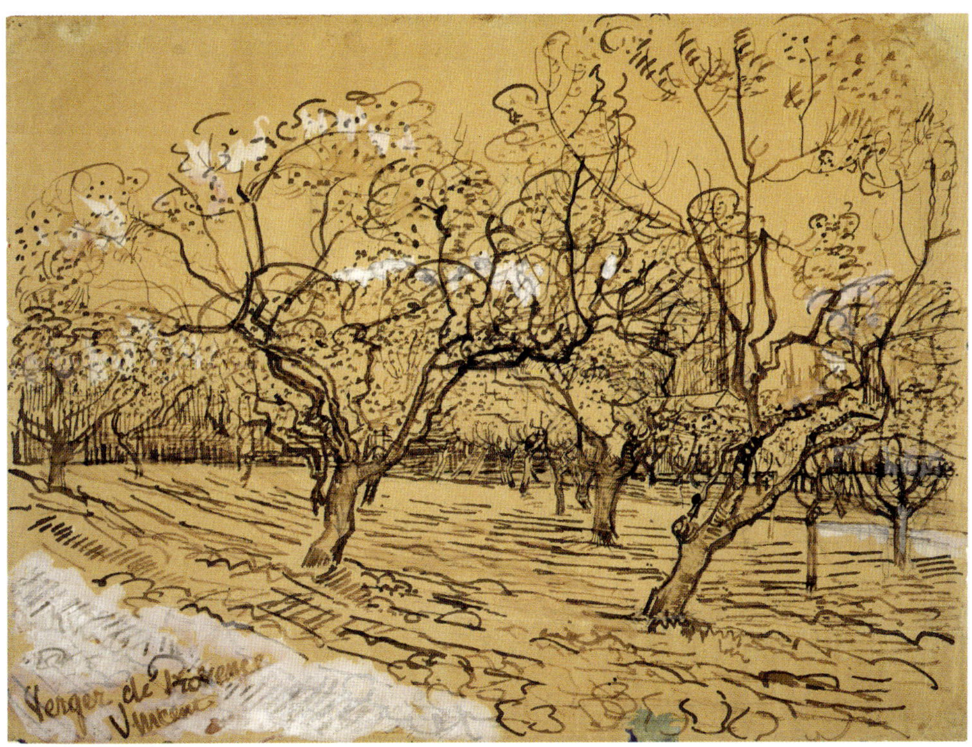

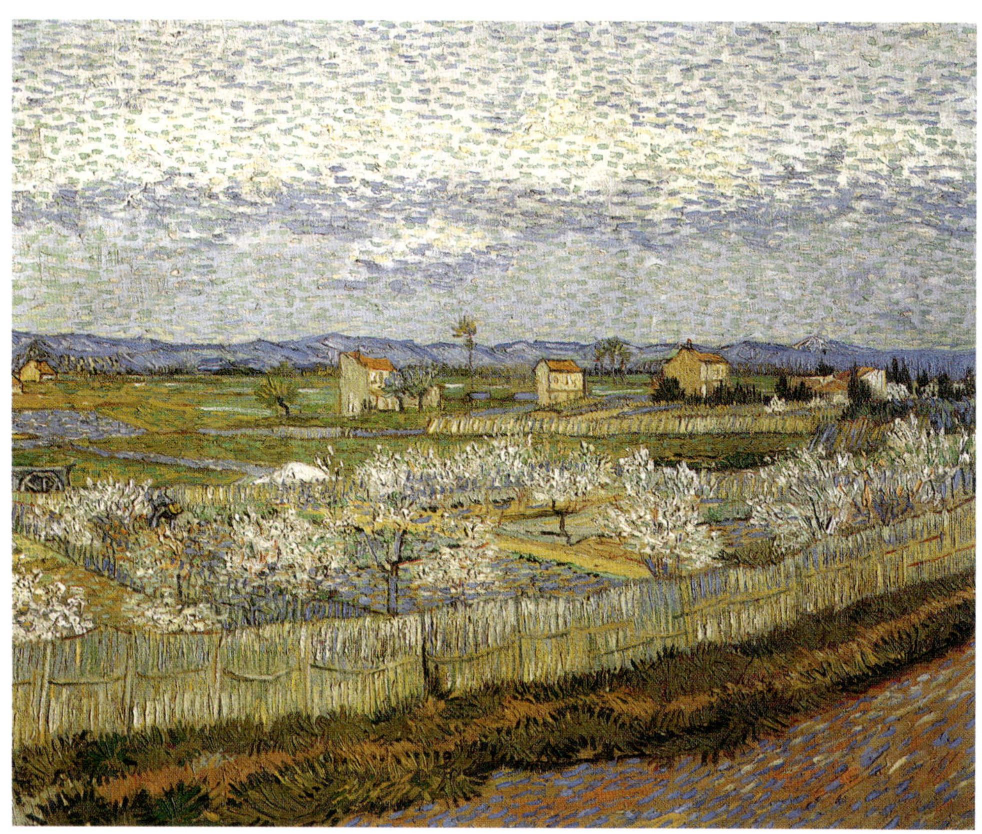

[56] *Peach Blossom in the Crau*
Arles, April 1889
Van Gogh used his own version
of the Pointillist technique to
portray the Crau, a plain located
a few kilometres east of Arles.
The small patches of brightly
coloured pigment animate the
picture surface to the extent that
the whole painting, not just the
peach orchards in the foreground,
seems to be blossoming. In a letter
to Paul Signac, Vincent described
the landscape as being made up
of particularly small elements –
gardens, fields, trees – 'even those
mountains, as in certain Japanese
landscapes, that's why this subject
attracted me' (756).

This 'fury' is hardly evident in the fourteen paintings – seven of which were in a vertical format and seven horizontal, which he hoped would facilitate some of the works being displayed as triptychs. Only a few have a bold, Expressionist character based on the use of impasto; most display Vincent's eclectic mix of Impressionist and Pointillist techniques to convey his impressions of the blossoming trees. Overall, the paintings illustrate his distinct talent for carefully crafted compositions where painting and drawing are subtly combined [53].

Vincent realized that there were sound commercial reasons for painting and drawing blossoming orchards. Firstly, the subject matter was known to be very popular with collectors. Secondly, these works might appeal to the artists with whom Vincent and Theo were already exchanging paintings and drawings with a view to augmenting their own collection: 'Orchards in blossom are subjects we have a chance of selling or exchanging' (594) [54].

During the period when Vincent was painting his series of flowering fruit trees, he received a letter from Wil enclosing Anton Mauve's obituary. Vincent had just returned from an orchard with a painting of 'two peach trees in full bloom, pink against a sparkling blue sky with white clouds and in sunshine' (590). Full of emotion he added 'Souvenir de Mauve' to the canvas, subsequently gifting it to his former tutor's widow, Jet. He also indicated that he had signed the work 'Vincent & Theo', but in fact Theo's name does not appear on the painting [55].

Vincent had hoped to resume his orchard paintings early in the spring of 1889. However, this venture was delayed considerably by his numerous mental crises and three hospitalizations in Arles between 24 December 1888 and 8 May 1889. The psychotic attacks were severe, but alternated with episodes of lucidity: 'In all I've had four big crises in which I hadn't the slightest idea of what I said, wanted, did' (764). In April 1889, during a calm period, he was allowed to paint outside the hospital and managed to create nine orchard paintings of great precision and radiance [56].

On Wednesday 8 May 1889, Vincent left Arles for the asylum of Saint-Paul-de-Mausole in Saint-Rémy, where

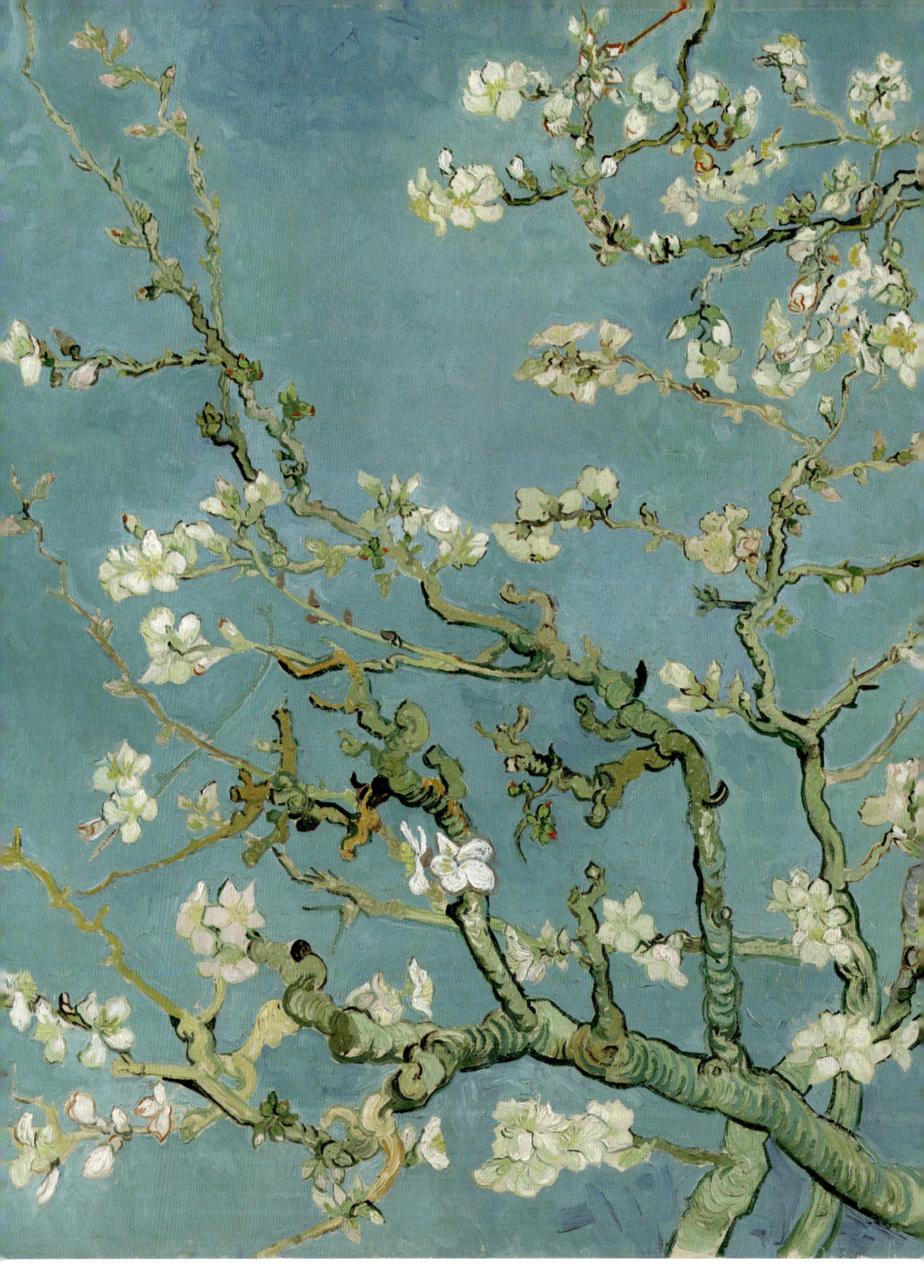

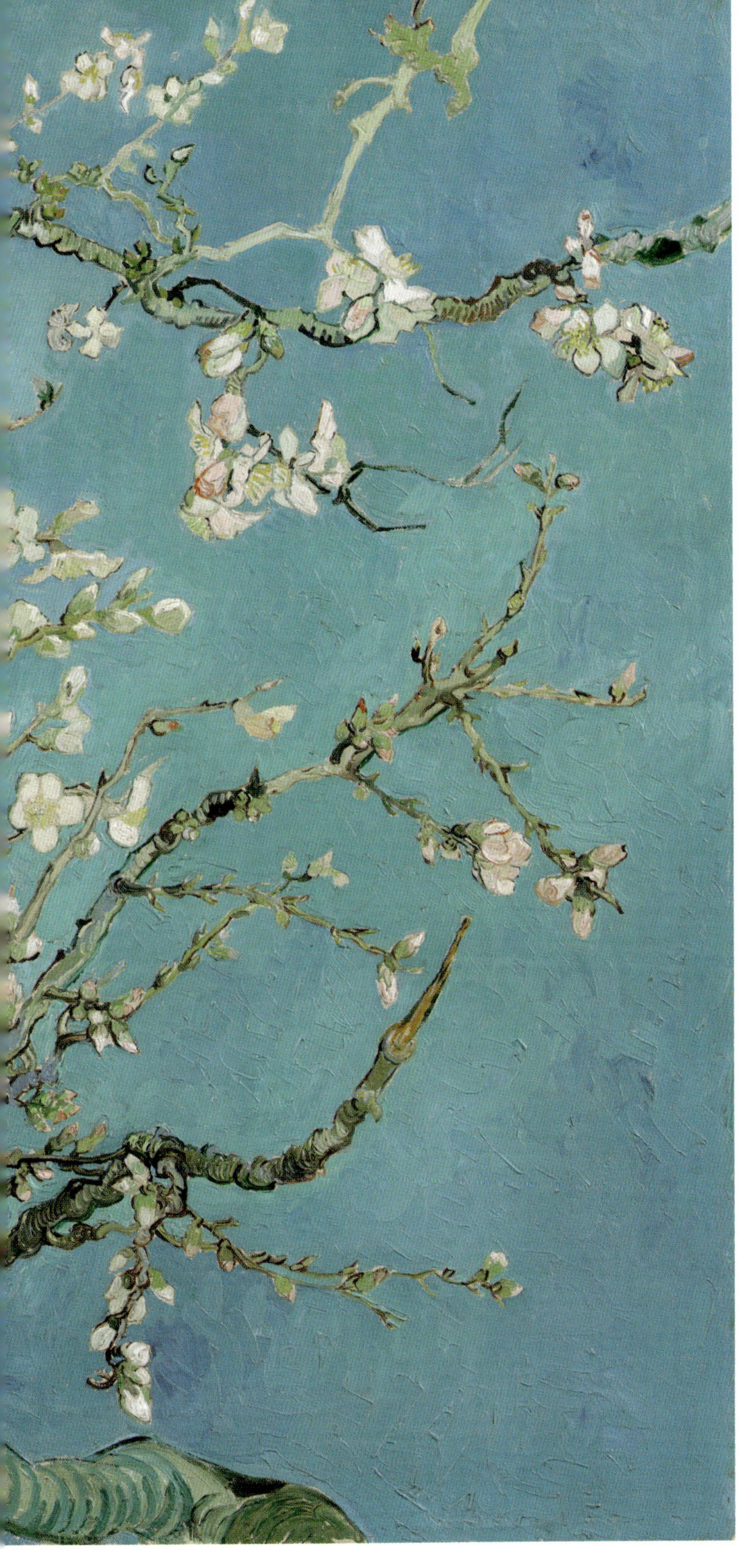

[57] *Branches with Almond Blossom*
Saint-Rémy, February 1890
The miracle of renewed life is
celebrated in this close-up view
of almond branches in flower.
The viewer's eye is drawn upwards
by the explosion of blossoms that
covers the whole picture plane.
This radiant canvas – the most
famous birthday present in art
history – has been painted with
great care in order to capture each
branch, twig, bud and flower. Sadly,
Vincent fell ill after completing
this painting and was unable to
work again for almost a month,
by which time only a few of the
orchards were still in bloom.

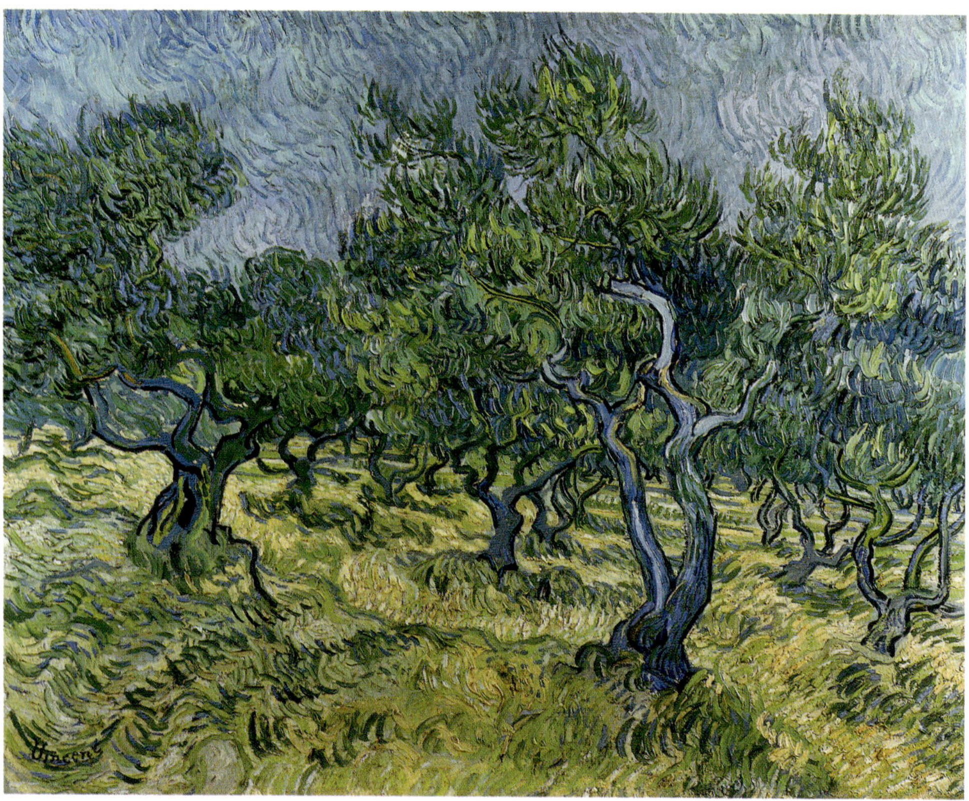

[58] *Olive Grove*
Saint-Rémy, mid-June 1889
In this painting, Vincent employed
rhythmic, flame-like brushstrokes to
represent the ground, trees and sky,
unifying the composition. Although
he relished the challenge of painting
the olive trees, he was acutely aware
of the technical problems he had to
face: 'But difficult, very difficult.
But that suits me...' (806).

he was to be a voluntary patient for a year. The following year,
in February 1890, on one of his walks beyond the asylum
walls, he was to paint his most famous, and most poignant,
image of a blossoming fruit tree. It was created to celebrate
the birth of his nephew, Vincent Willem, the son of his
brother Theo, and Theo's wife, Jo (Johanna van Gogh-Bonger,
1862–1925). Symbolizing new life, the picture seems to have
been achieved by a paradoxical combination of precision and
exuberance [57].

Although all his paintings of olive orchards and groves
were produced during his stay at the asylum in Saint-Rémy,
Vincent had first seen the potential of these trees as subject
matter in April 1889, while still living in Arles: 'Ah, my dear
Theo, if you could see the olive trees at this time of year' (763).
But he felt that he could not do justice to the subtlety and
refinement of the olive tree: 'It's too beautiful for me to

dare paint it or be able to form an idea of it' (763). Two months later, however, he embarked on a series of fifteen canvases, of which the first group was completed in June 1889, with the remainder painted in the autumn months. The colours of the olive leaves reminded him of the willow trees that he had painted in the Netherlands; but it was the blue sky of Provence that seemed to make the muted colours of the olive trees so distinctive. He became fascinated by the 'old-silver and silver foliage greening up against the blue' (763) [58]. Indeed, he hoped that this colour and tonal scheme might form the basis of a group of related works, similar to what he had achieved in Arles with his sunflower paintings, which were based on tones of yellow and orange.

When he was painting and drawing the groves, it was not only the forms and colours of the olive trees that impressed

[59] *Olive Trees: Montmajour*
Pencil, quill and reed pen with brown and black ink
Arles, July 1888
Vincent used elaborate patterns of calligraphy marks to represent the slight breeze in the olive grove. While living in the Netherlands, Vincent had described his response to similar woodland scenes: 'I see that nature has told me something, has spoken to me and that I've written it down in shorthand' (260).

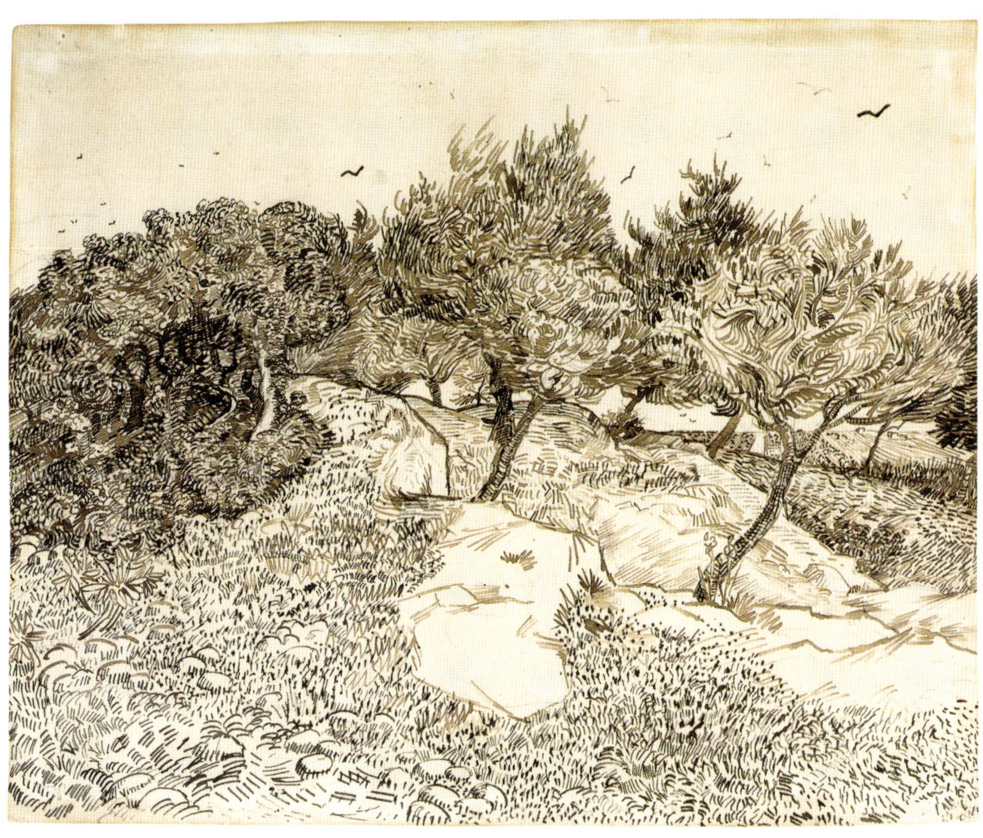

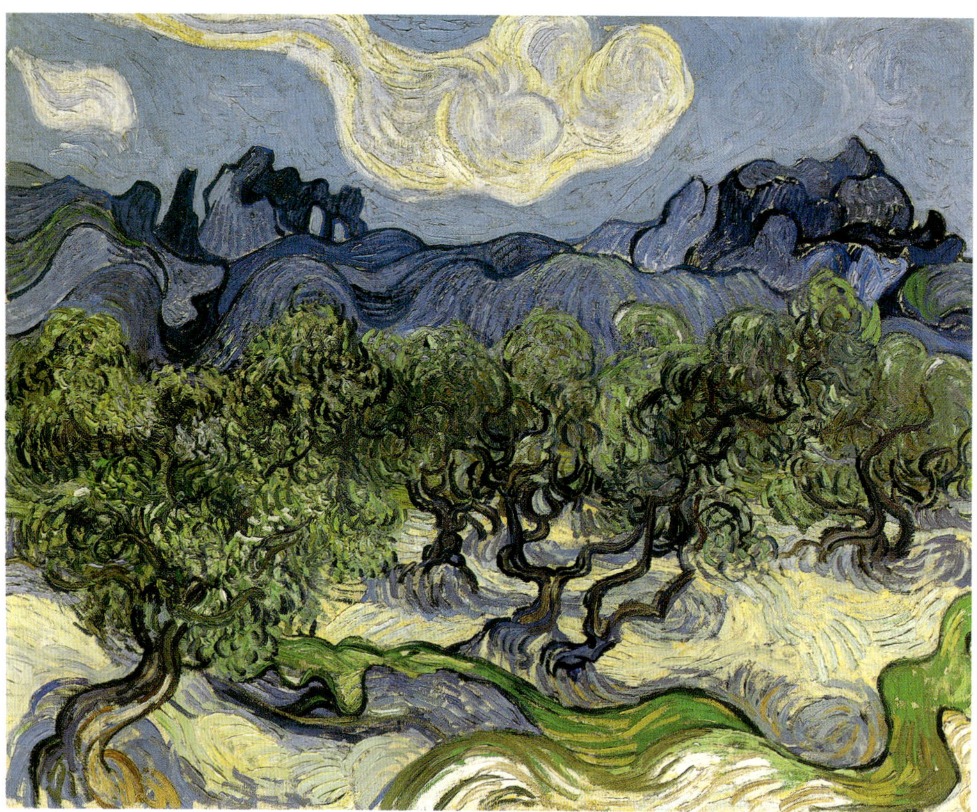

[60] *Olive Trees with the Alpilles in the Background*
Saint-Rémy, mid-June 1889
In this painting, Van Gogh deliberately stylized the groundscape, trees, hills and clouds to give the image expressive force. He believed that the resulting forms were 'contorted like those of the ancient woodcuts'. Parallel lines or 'striations' were used to suggest movement across the picture plane, a device Vincent particularly favoured: 'Where these lines are close together and deliberate, the painting begins, even if it may be exaggerated' (805).

him, but also the hypnotic rustle of their leaves: 'The murmur of an olive grove has something very intimate, intensely old about it' (763) [59]. Although Vincent perceived a Provençal olive grove to be 'a thing of such delicacy – so refined' (763), in some of his landscapes he deliberately exaggerated the forms of trees, fields, hills and clouds – he hoped to achieve more intense, timeless images in this way [60]. While his paintings of blossoming orchards are, as he intended, joyful and reassuring works, the olive grove canvases seem to be more mysterious and contemplative in mood. Interestingly, none of the olive grove paintings shows the trees in flower. Vincent relished the richer tones of the sunlit landscape in the autumn months of 1889, with the olive trees casting their long shadows [61]. In the Netherlands, he had painted many avenues at sunset; now he could explore the light qualities of dusk as it affected the deserted groves [62].

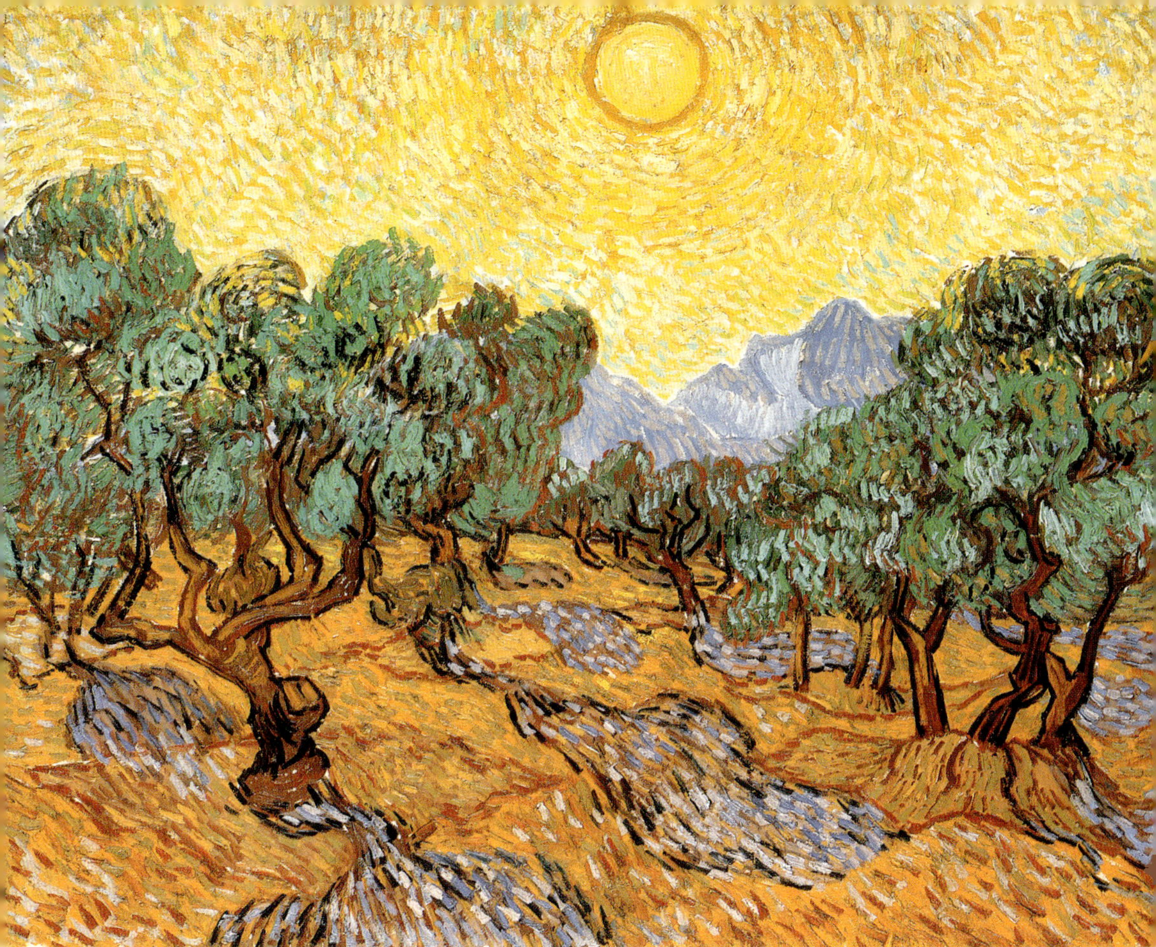

[61] *Olive Trees with Yellow Sky and Sun*
Saint-Rémy, November 1889
Surprisingly, this is the only painting in the olive grove series to include 'a big yellow sun' (827). Centrally placed in the golden sky and touching the top of the picture plane, the sun dominates the composition both formally and in terms of the warm colour scheme.

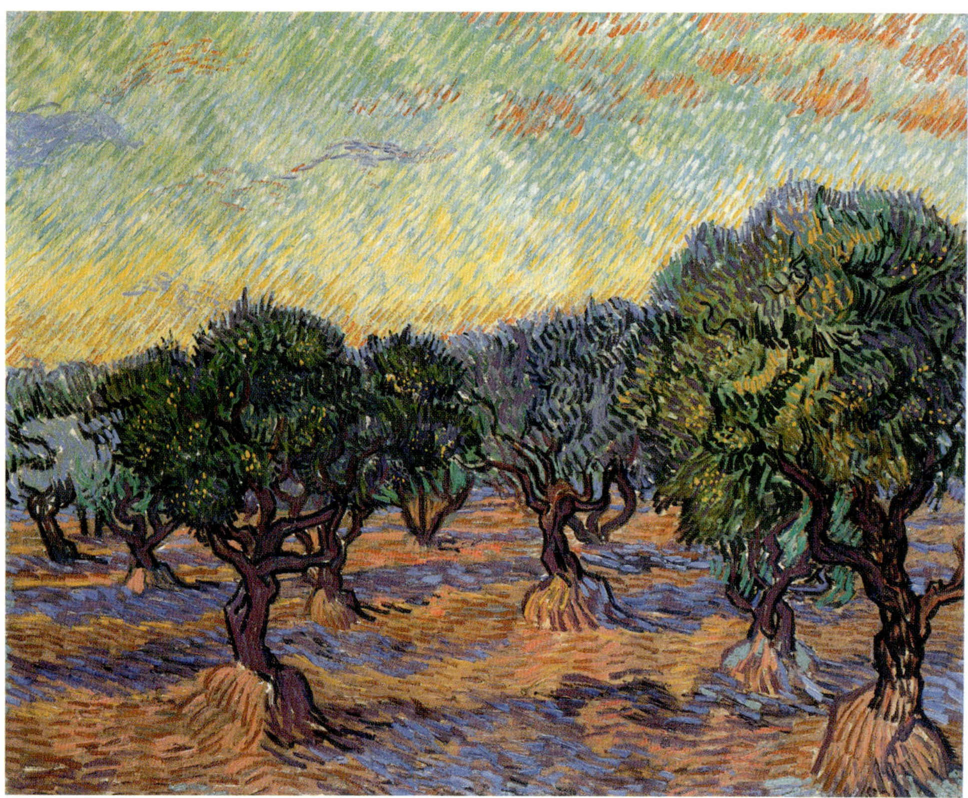

In December 1889, Vincent completed four studies of female workers picking olives in the groves. Although he did not wish to emulate his friends Bernard and Gauguin in painting canvases based on the theme of Christ in the Garden of Olives, he did acknowledge that his images of olive picking might have religious connotations for some people [63]. However, he was adamant that he would not undertake an overtly Christian painting within an olive-grove setting. The *Garden of Olives* paintings by Bernard and Gauguin were flawed, he believed, because the two artists had not based their decorative improvisations on a preliminary analysis of an authentic location: 'Friend Bernard has probably never seen an olive tree' (820). Compared to Bernard and Gauguin, Vincent was much more interested in a direct response to nature, thereby producing less esoteric, stylized imagery than his two friends: 'What I've done is a rather harsh

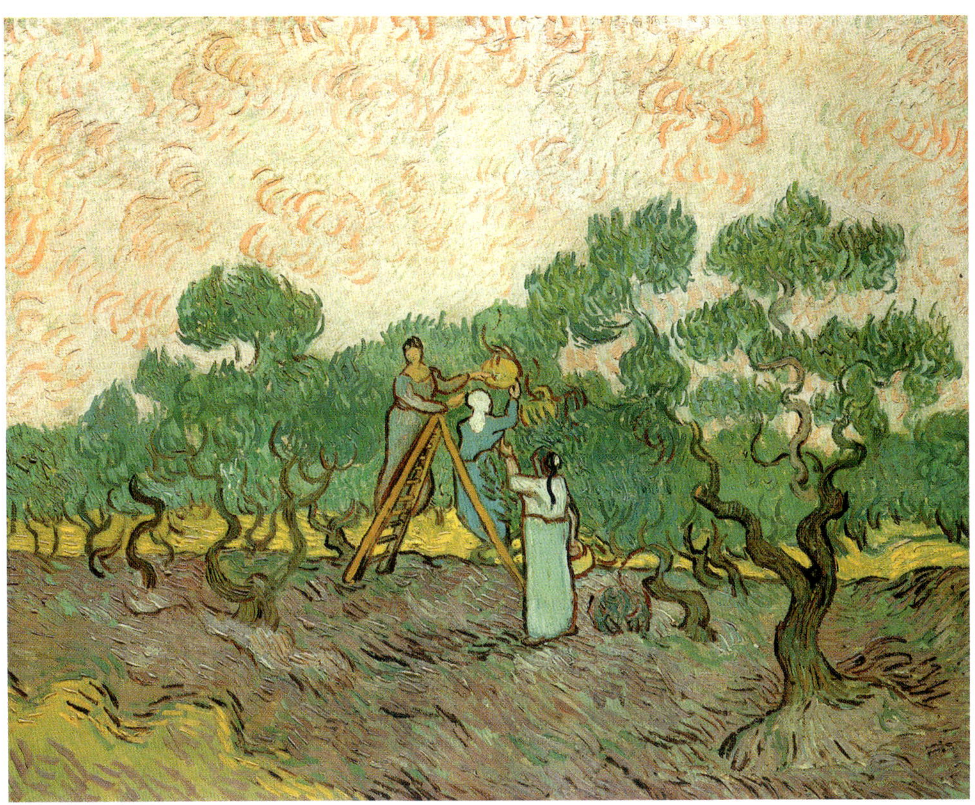

and coarse realism beside their abstractions, but it will nevertheless impart the rustic note, and will smell of the soil' (823).

[63] *Olive Picking*
Saint-Rémy, December 1889
While none of Vincent's paintings of blossoming orchards includes figures, four of his images of olive groves show women picking olives. The harvesting theme concurs with Van Gogh's interest in representing the cycle of the seasons in his work.

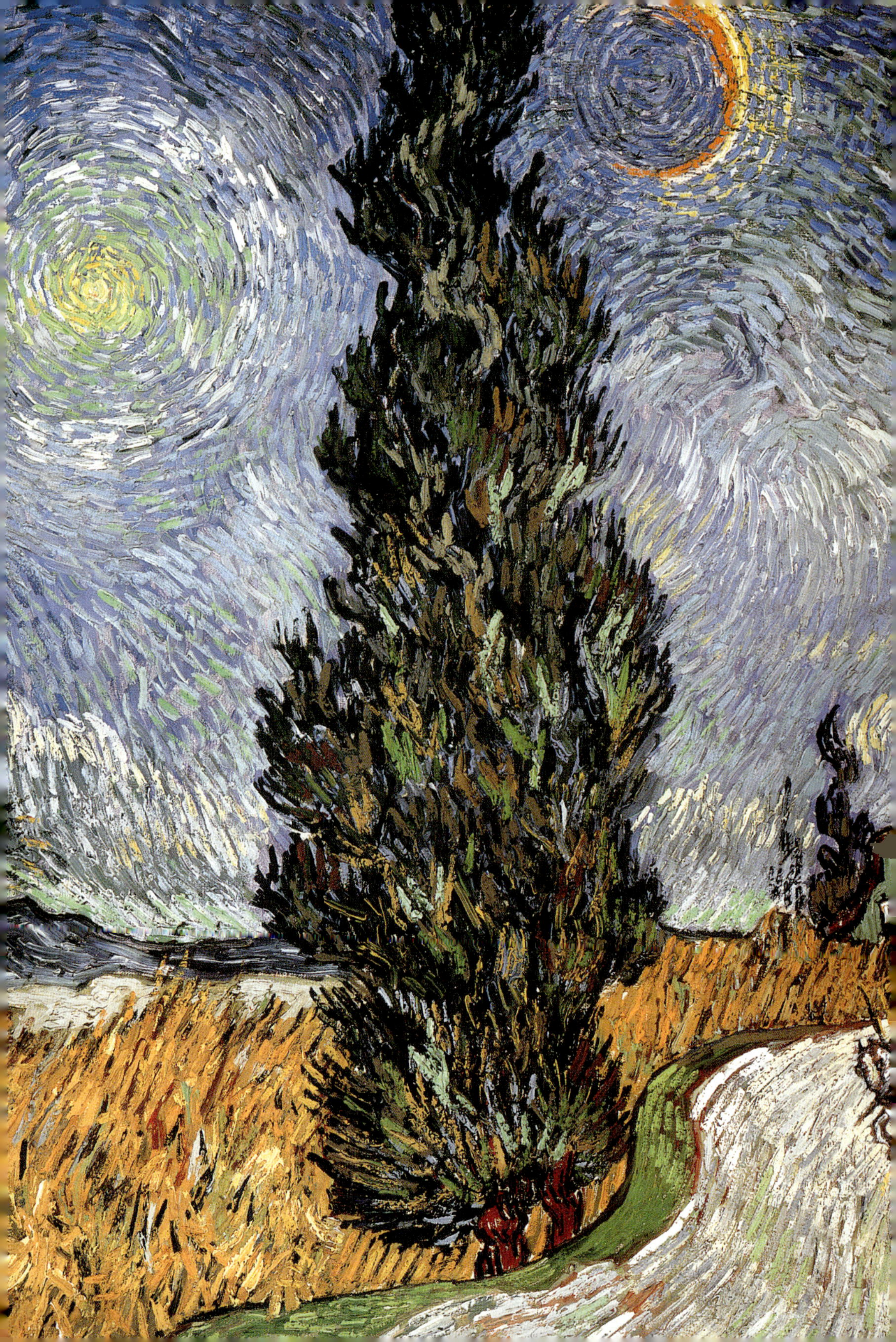

CHAPTER 5

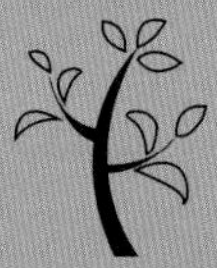

Vincent's Provençal Trees

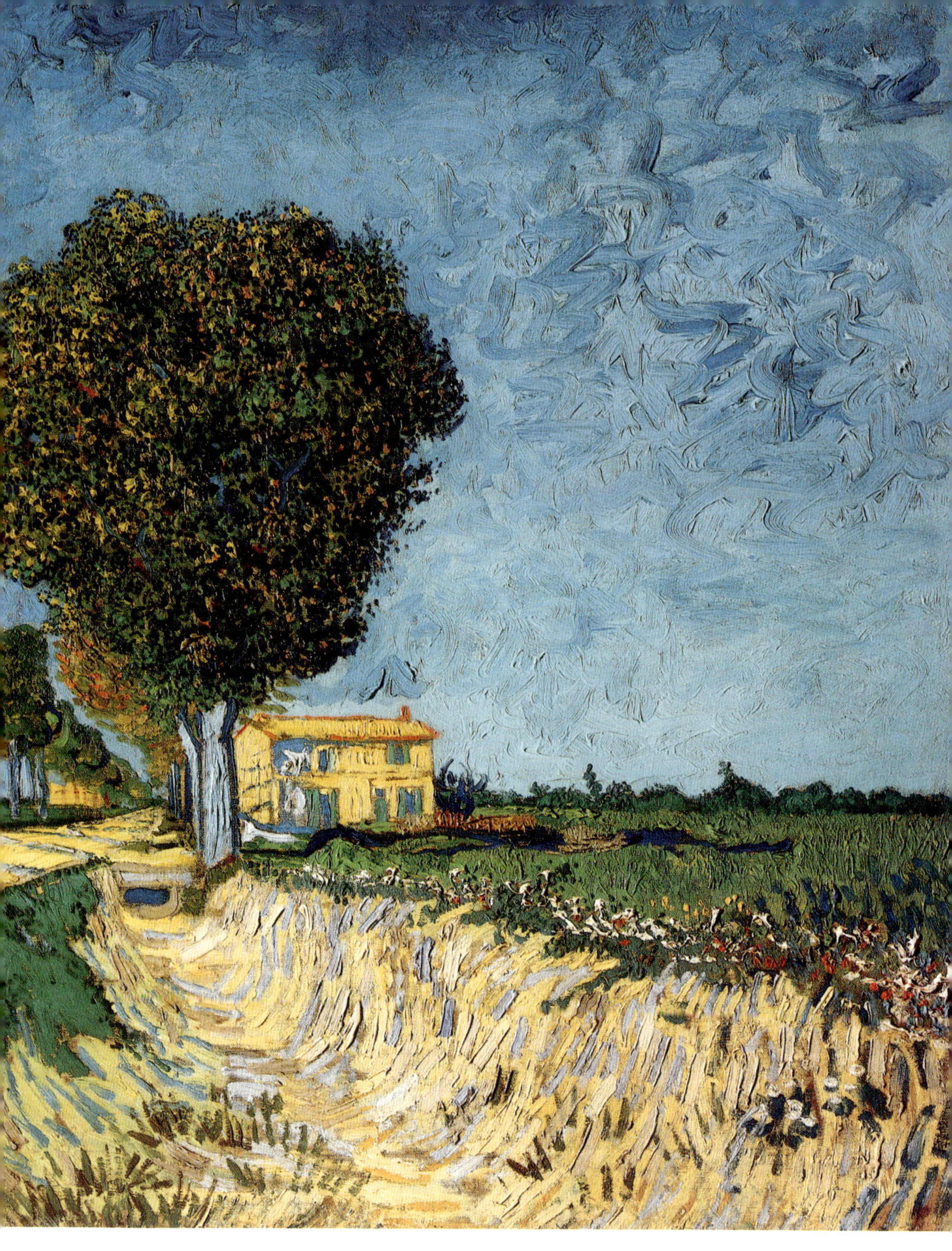

'Now, *better than in the beginning,*
I see the real countryside of Provence…'

Vincent understood that 'the real countryside of Provence' was an amalgam of many different components: not only hills, fields, orchards and trees, but also agricultural elements, vernacular buildings and, above all, the pervasive quality of the light. It was this total vision of a distinctive environment that he hoped to achieve in his paintings and drawings of Provence: 'For yes, one must feel the wholeness of a country' (816). In fact, he wondered whether the work he created in the south of France might not constitute an integrated body of images, which he referred to as 'Impressions of Provence' (808).

Van Gogh's habit of undertaking long country walks, wherever he was living, continued in Provence. While he was based in Arles, these walks along country lanes provided him with important insights into the landscape, the brightness of the colours and the purity of the light: 'What strikes me here, and what makes painting here attractive to me, is the clarity of the air' (626) [64]. As a consequence, most of his country walks became painting and drawing expeditions. His self-imposed challenge of representing bright sunlight using only the ink-drawing medium resulted in a highly original notation [65]. On these walks, Vincent sometimes discovered unusual rural places that stimulated his literary imagination. A stony heath, where small twisted oaks were growing, he perceived as particularly Romantic and imagined as the setting for a medieval pageant. The resulting painting, completed outdoors, shows a centrally placed oak tree that lends the image an emblematic character [66]. The canvas also reveals Vincent's admiration for the Provençal artist Adolphe Joseph Thomas Monticelli (1824–1886), who was renowned for his picturesque scenes and bold painting technique.

Walking three miles northeast of Arles, Van Gogh could reach Montmajour, a small rocky place on a hill covered with

[64] *A Lane near Arles*
Arles, May 1888
In this work, Provençal farmhouses nestle beside the kind of tree-lined lane that Vincent loved to paint. He stated that he never tired of the blue Provence sky, the feature that dominates this painting, and he believed that 'by intensifying *all* the colours, one again achieves calm and harmony' (590).

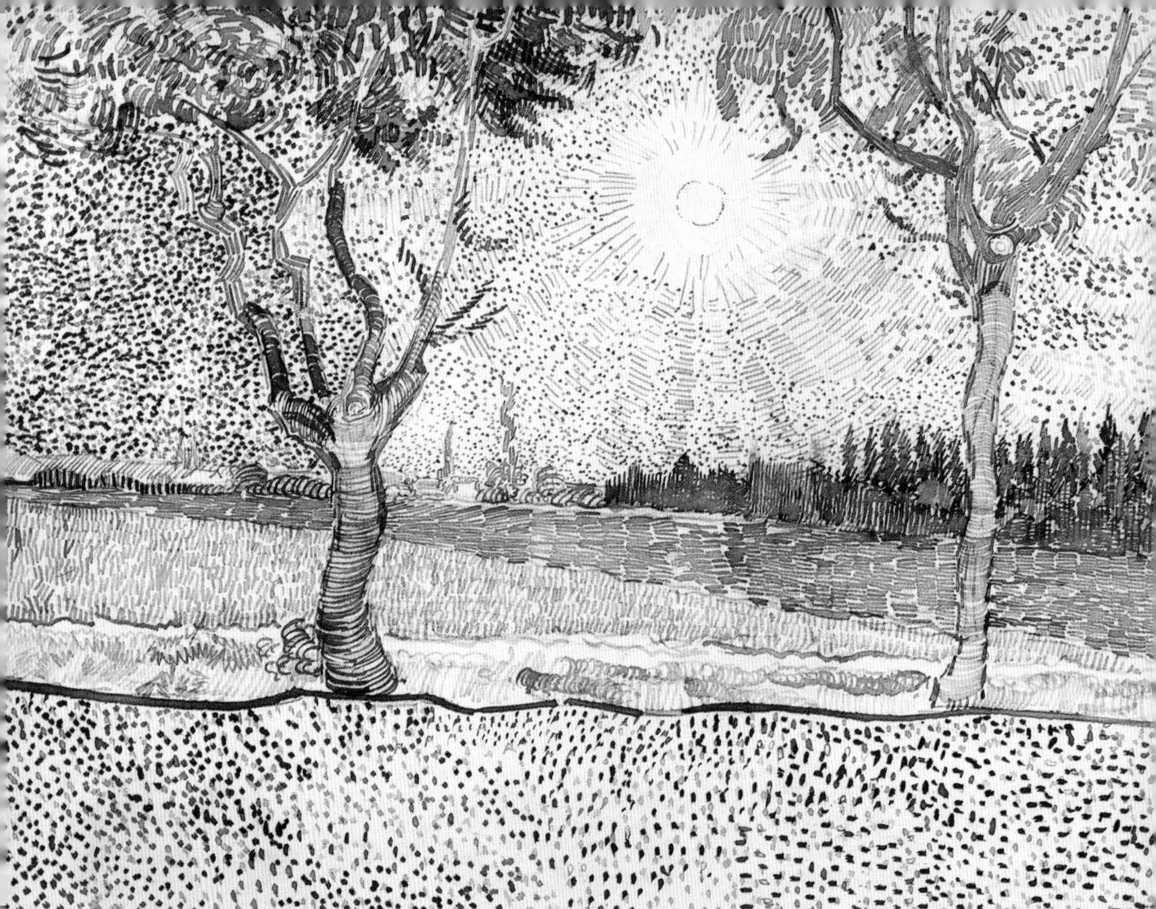

[65] *The Road to Tarascon*
(for John Russell)

Reed pen, pen and ink over
graphite on wove paper

Arles, July–August 1888

Vincent sometimes transferred his
Pointillist style of painting to the
medium of drawing. Here, using
a vocabulary of tiny ink marks, he
created a diverse landscape bathed
in sunlight. The sky and the road
seem equally bright, and the two trees
are like sentinels guarding the sun.

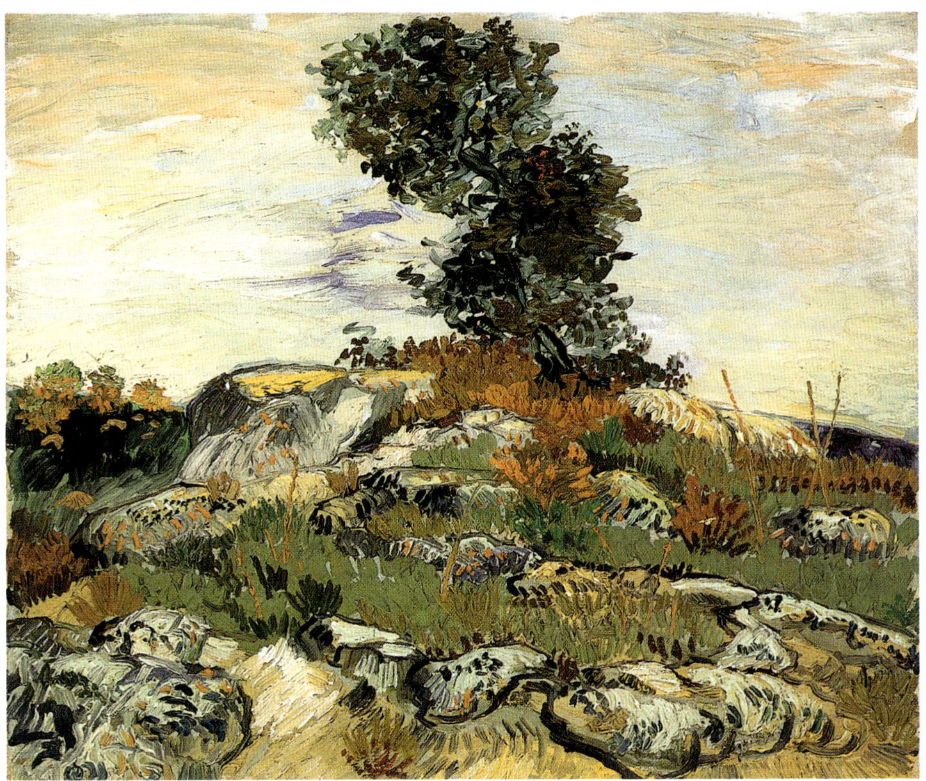

holly, olives and pines. With its ruined abbey, it presented
him with a dramatic vantage point for his numerous
panoramic views of the surrounding countryside, including
the agricultural hinterland of Arles. One of Vincent's most
famous drawings, reminiscent of the landscape compositions
created by seventeenth-century Dutch masters such as
Jacob van Ruisdael (*c.* 1628–1682), depicts a 'group of very
dark pines and the town of Arles in the background' (639).
He was intrigued by how the pines in the foreground seemed
to be clinging to the rocky outcrop and how the road in the
distance, like those of his homeland, was lined with poplars
[67]. Exhibited and purchased in 1893, just three years after
his death, this was the first Van Gogh drawing to enter
a public collection.

It was not just the poplar trees of Provence that reminded
him of the Netherlands. To his surprise, he also encountered

[66] *Rocks with Oak Tree*
Arles, July 1888
Van Gogh greatly admired landscape
paintings by seventeenth-century
Dutch artists who chose trees as
major focal points. Writing to
Theo in October 1885, he expressed
his enthusiasm for the painting
Landscape with Oaks by Jan van
Goyen (1596–1656). Vincent's own
painting can be seen as continuing
this Dutch tradition.

pollard willows, the much admired features of Brabant, growing in the meadows of Provence. In his new paintings of these trees, Vincent emphasized the startling colours of the southern landscape [68]; he believed that he had achieved greater expressive power by using colour in a less naturalistic manner: 'Because instead of trying to render exactly what I have before my eyes, I use colour more arbitrarily in order to express myself forcefully' (663). In addition, the bright colours that surrounded him on his walks in the Provençal countryside almost led him to imagine that he was moving through a sequence of Japanese block prints, with their pure colours and clearly outlined forms. Vincent explained: 'I don't need Japanese prints here, because I'm always saying to myself that *I am in Japan here*' (678). An examination of some of his tree paintings, for instance *The Old Yew*, reveals the

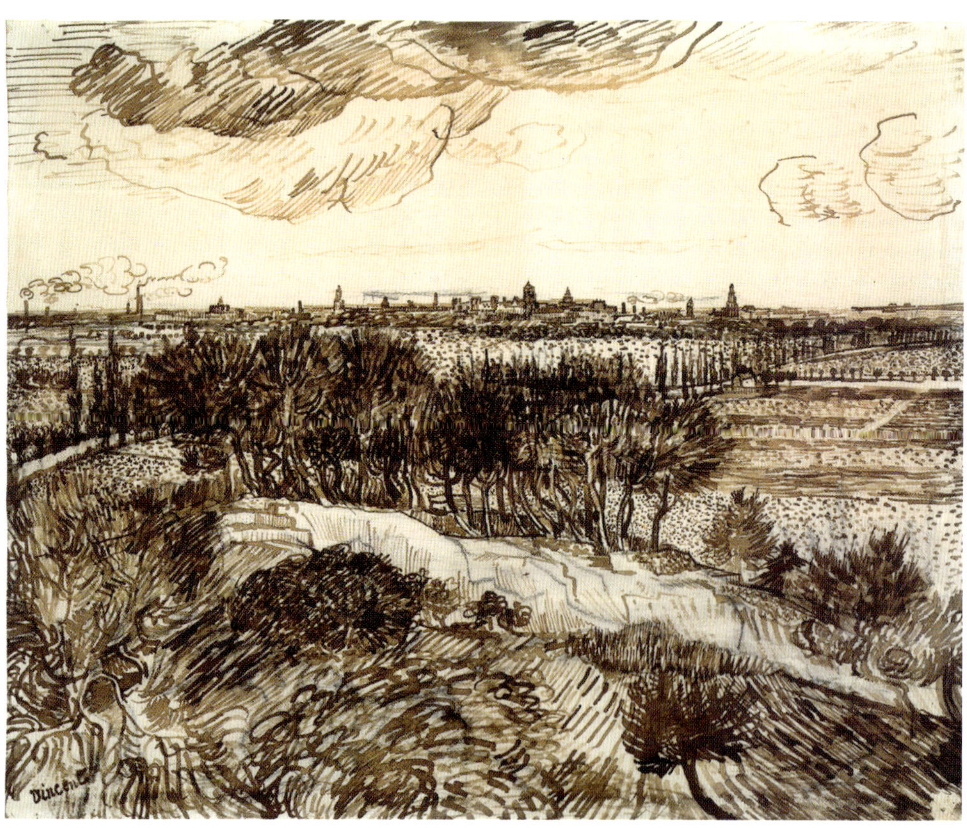

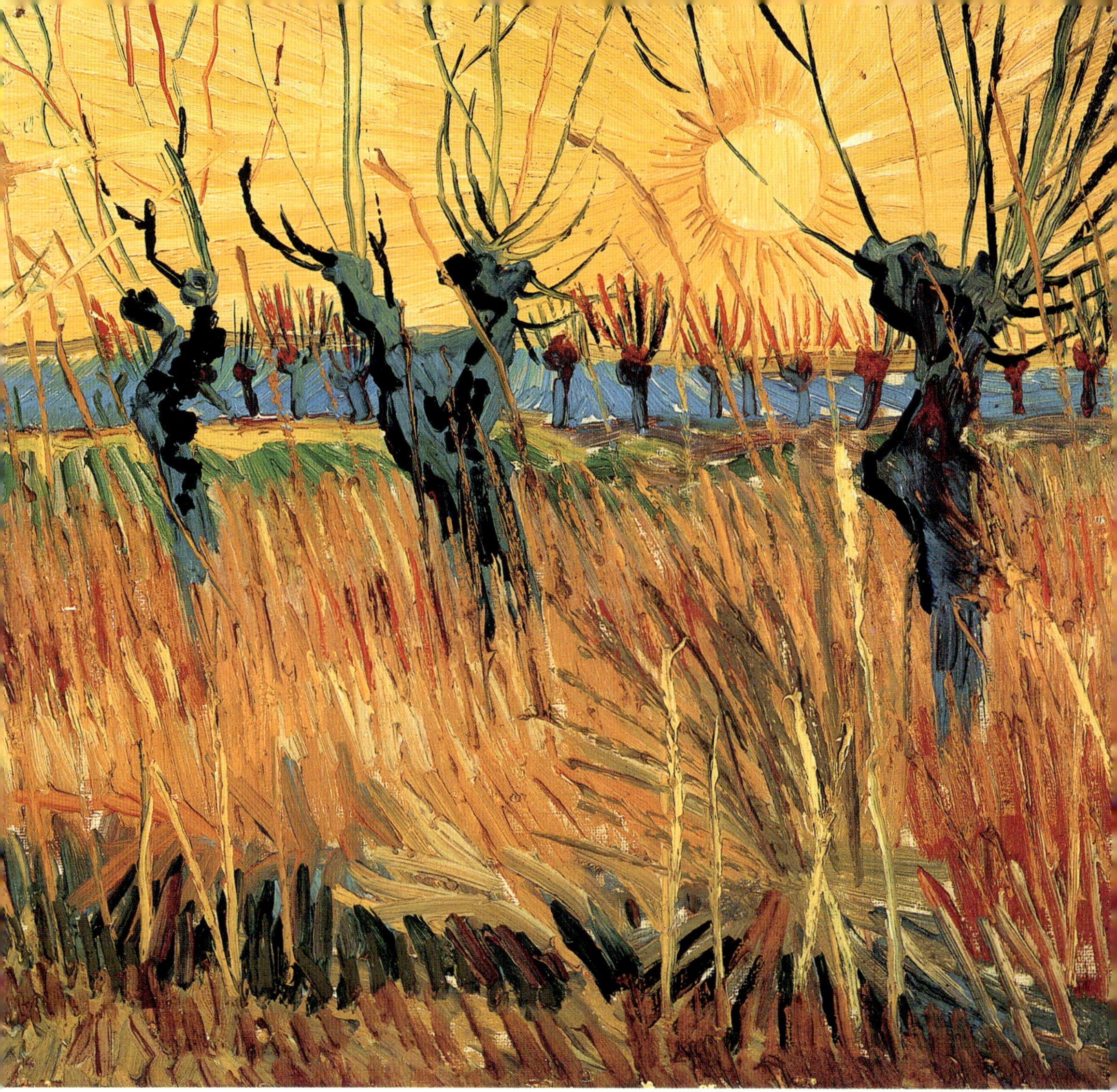

[68] *Willows at Sunset*
Arles, Autumn 1888
This small painting has a powerful
presence. The imagery is familiar –
tortured trees and setting sun – but
the colour scheme has been reduced
to an intense combination of gold
and blue. Vincent, always keen
to theorize, declared regarding
this set of complementary colours:
'NO BLUE WITHOUT YELLOW
and WITHOUT ORANGE, and if you
do blue, then do yellow and orange
as well, surely' (622).

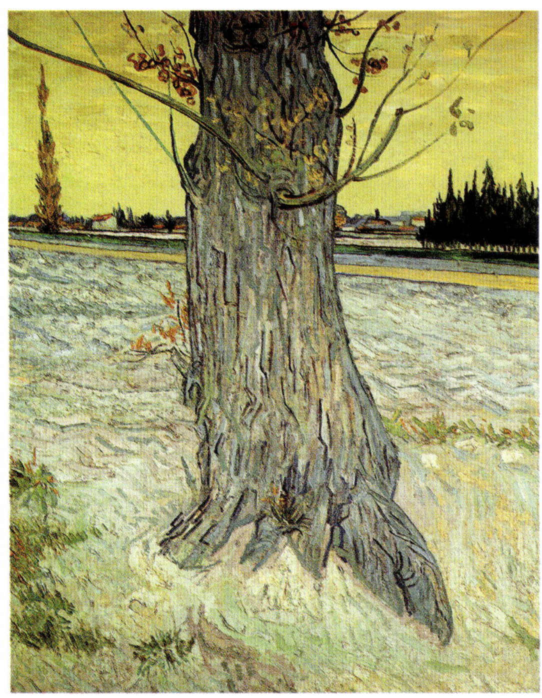

influence of Japanese prints in terms of composition, drawing and colour harmony [69].

When Van Gogh first arrived at the asylum at Saint-Rémy in May 1889, he was not allowed to undertake his customary countryside walks for about a month because of his delicate mental state. Fortunately, he was permitted to work in the overgrown walled garden, where he was to paint some of his most famous flower studies. It was in the asylum garden (or 'park', as he called it) that Vincent rediscovered one of his favourite tree species — the pine. His fondness for pines had been fostered during childhood walks in the woods of Brabant; now, in this Provençal garden, he became fascinated by the groups of statuesque pine trees, with their distinctive russet trunks and branches, and their dark green foliage set against the pure blue sky. As these tall trees were such dominant features of asylum complex, Vincent decided to present a painting of them to the asylum director, Théophile Peyron (1827–1895). Interestingly, in some paintings of the walled garden Vincent attempted to reconstruct the

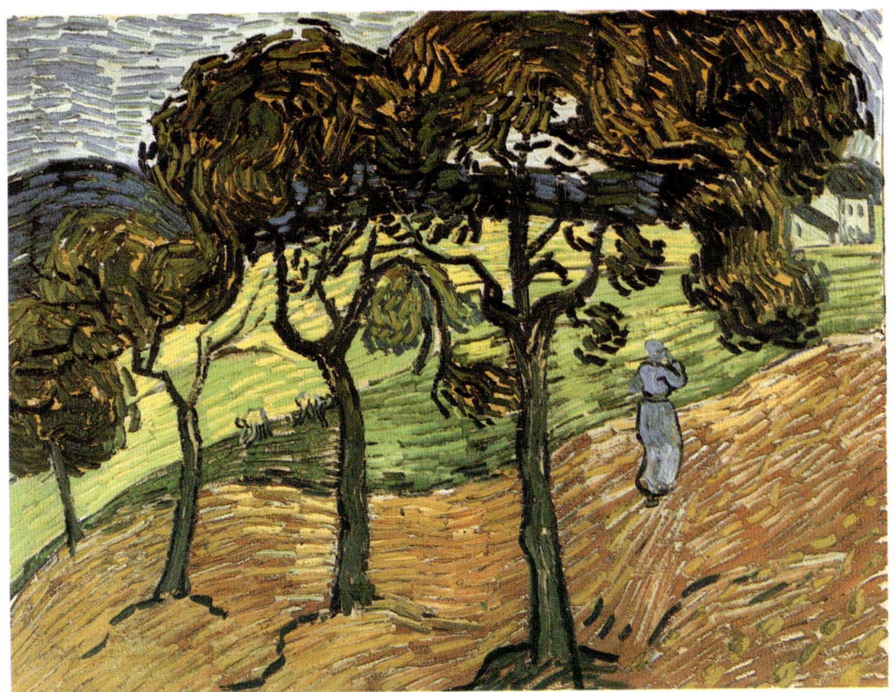

essence of the place 'by simplifying and accentuating
the proud, unchanging nature of the pines' (810).

When Vincent was allowed to venture outside the asylum
complex, under supervision, he produced memorable
drawings and paintings of the pine trees that were growing
along the country lanes and around the fields [70] [71].
Remarkably, using only a limited range of lines in black chalk,
he created a series of very expressive graphic images. In
Arles he had often felt that his paintings lacked the vigorous
interwoven brushwork that he desired due to the disruption
caused by the mistral. Some of his pine-tree paintings made
in Saint-Rémy, however, possess 'brushstrokes that hold
together and intertwine well, with feeling, like a piece of
music played with emotion' (691).

When he walked further away from the asylum, Vincent
encountered a species of tree that he came to view as
particularly characteristic of the Provençal landscape – the
cypress. During his painting excursions in the fields and hills
surrounding Saint-Rémy, the brightness of the sky seemed

[70] *Landscape with
Trees and Figures*
Saint-Rémy, November 1889
The coloured striations in this
painting create an overall pattern
that is reminiscent of a woven
fabric. The four giant pine trees
and the two enigmatic figures
are combined in a composition
of great psychological intensity.

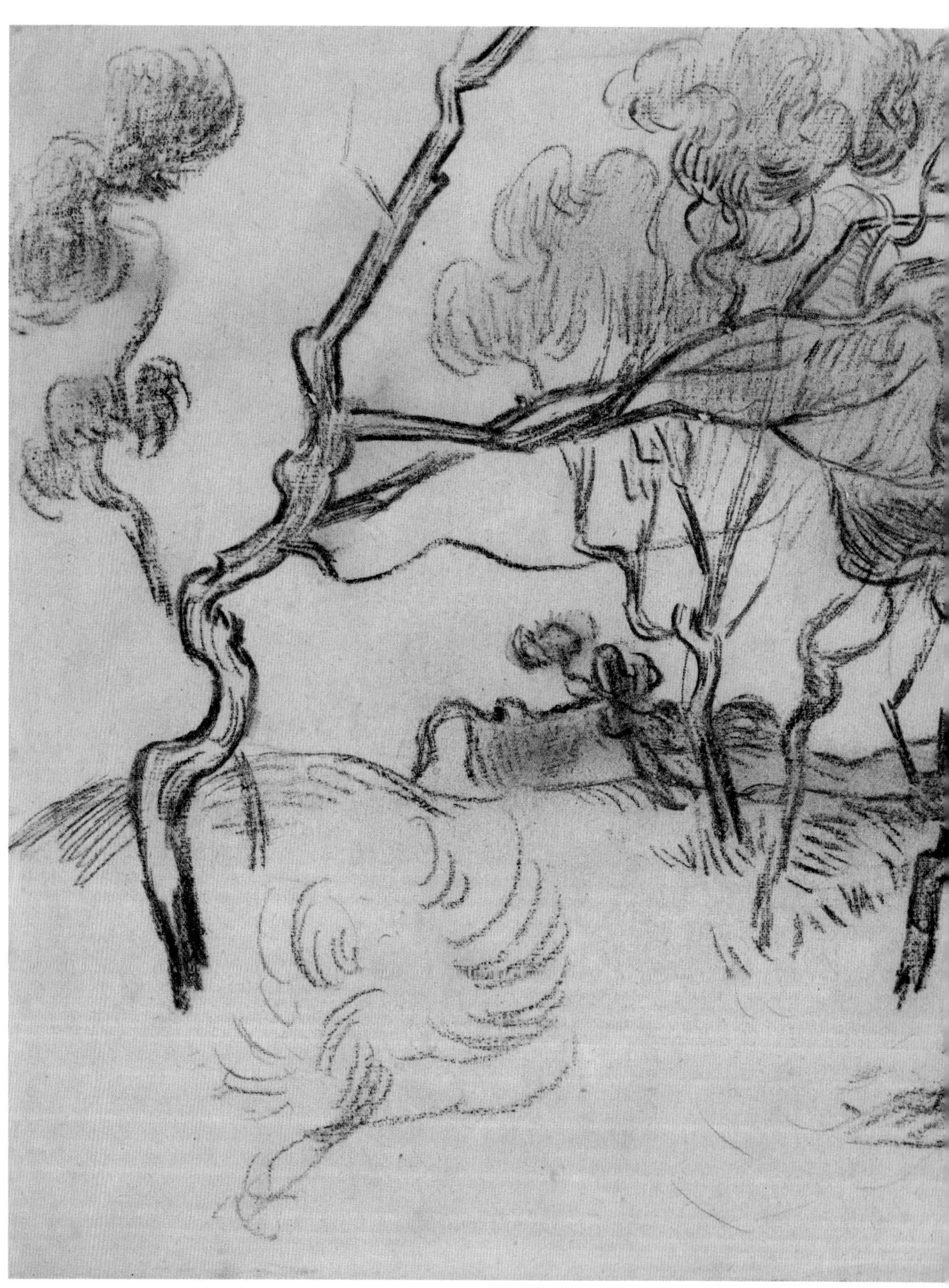

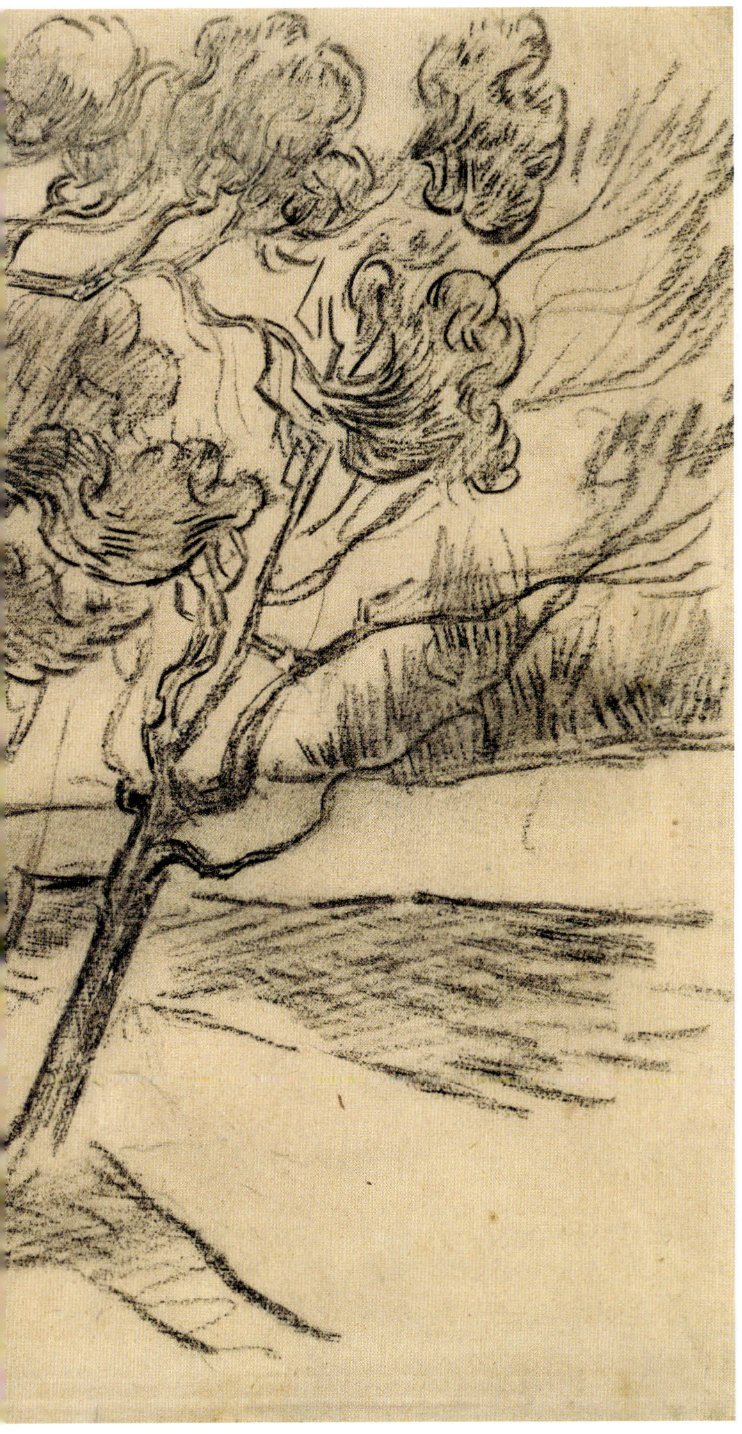

[71] *Road with Pine Trees*
Black chalk (stumped)
Saint-Rémy, May–October 1889
As in many of Van Gogh's drawings,
the subject is carefully observed yet
represented with great forcefulness.

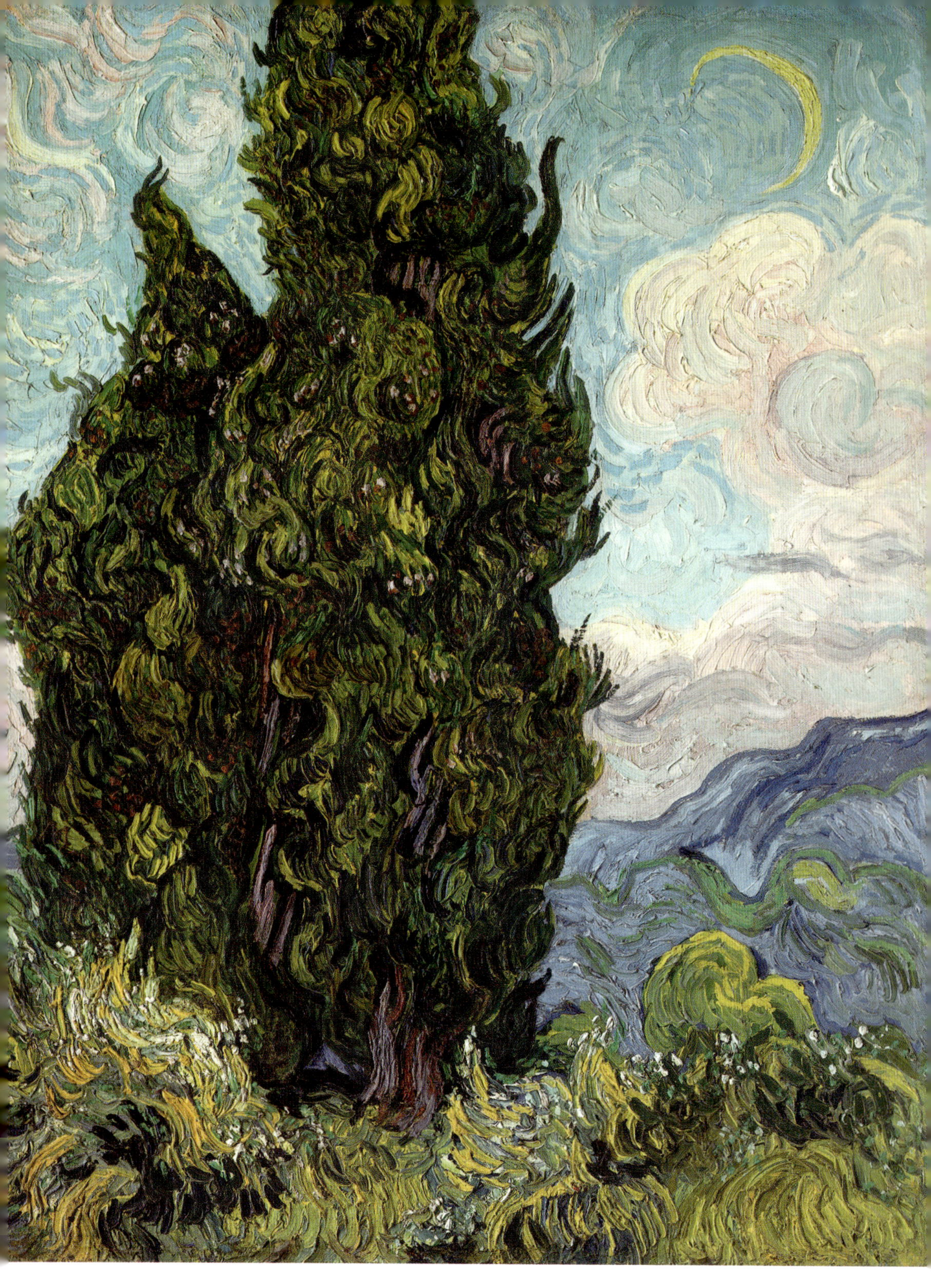

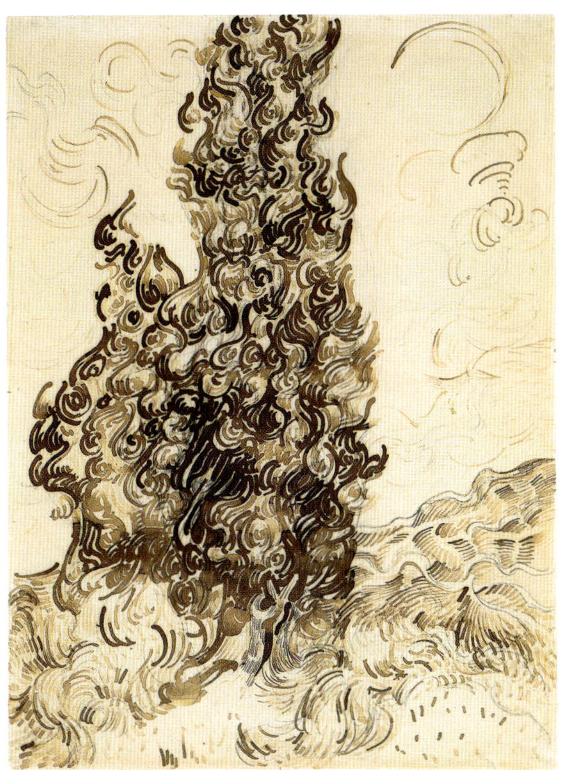

to envelop the cypresses; indeed, he did not perceive them
as being set against the blue sky but 'in the blue rather' (783).
Significantly, Vincent did not believe that any other artist
had yet managed to capture their 'flame-like' forms (850)
and he became preoccupied with depicting their distinctive
vertical presence in the landscape. Portraying the cypresses'
dark green forms against the parched vista was particularly
demanding, but resulted in original paintings [72]. Vincent
also discovered that his highly individual approach to ink
drawing could be used effectively to convey the complex
movement patterns of the leaves and branches that occurred
when the cypresses were buffeted by the mistral [73].

Vincent told Theo of his increasing fascination with the
cypress tree, especially its black-green silhouette within
the sunny landscape: 'It's beautiful as regards lines and
proportions, like an Egyptian obelisk. And the green has
such a distinguished quality' (783). Some of his most famous

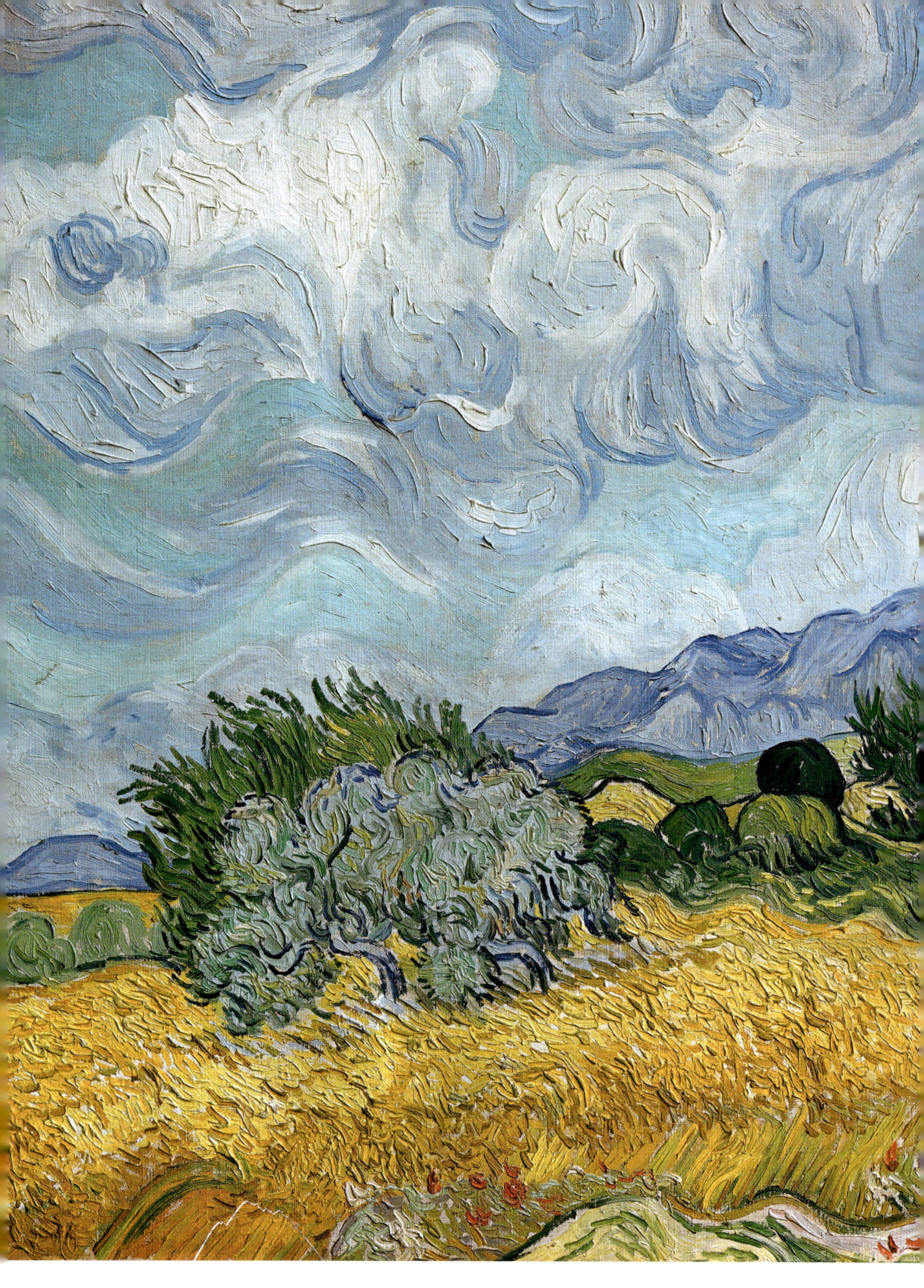

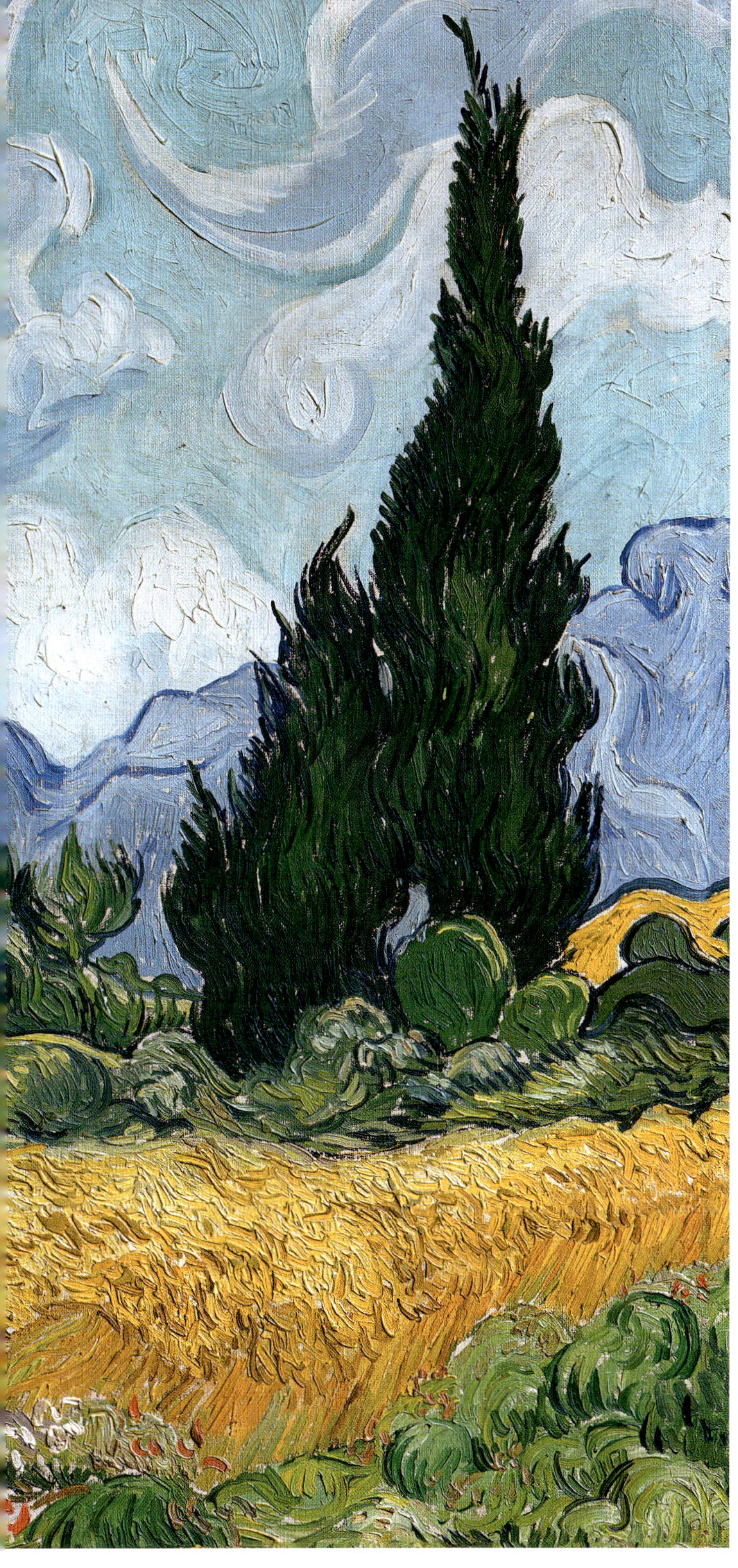

[74] *A Wheatfield with Cypresses*
Saint-Rémy, early September 1889
The black-green colour of the
cypresses is the crucial feature
in this composition: 'It's the *dark*
patch in a sun-drenched landscape,
but it's one of the most interesting
dark notes, the most difficult to hit
off exactly that I can imagine' (783).

landscapes explore these formal and colour qualities, and present the cypress tree as a memorable symbol of Provence [74].

Vincent did not object to painting from memory as a matter of principle; he believed, however, that such a practice should be preceded by many studies from nature. He did acknowledge that sometimes 'the canvases done from memory have a more artistic look' (718) and also noticed that such imaginative improvisations could take on a more mysterious character than naturalistic studies. One of his most successful and poetic compositions was painted from memory and used a cypress tree as key motif [75]. In this painting, Vincent created an image which seems to be, on the one hand, an evocation of his moods and memories, and on the other, a portrayal of a particular place. Writing to Paul Gauguin about the canvas, he summed up this duality: 'Very romantic if you like, but also "Provençal" I think' (RM23). Thus, 'the real countryside of Provence' had been distilled into one enigmatic painting.

Van Gogh viewed the series of cypress paintings as complementary to the sunflower canvases he had completed in Arles. In his imagination, both the cypress tree and the sunflower had come to represent the essence of Provence, and he thought that his paintings of sunflowers and cypress trees could one day epitomize his unique vision. Since his death in 1890, these two motifs have indeed come to be recognized by many as the quintessential emblems of his work as a painter.

In November 1883, when he had less than seven years left to live, Vincent set out his aim as an artist: 'My plan for my life is to make paintings and drawings, as many and as well as I can' (405). However, he also mused on his likely feelings when nearing death: 'Then, when my life is over, I hope to depart in no other way than looking back with love and wistfulness and thinking, oh paintings that I would have made!' (405). While sympathizing with his sentiments, one can only marvel at the spectacular paintings that he did manage to complete in such a short period of time.

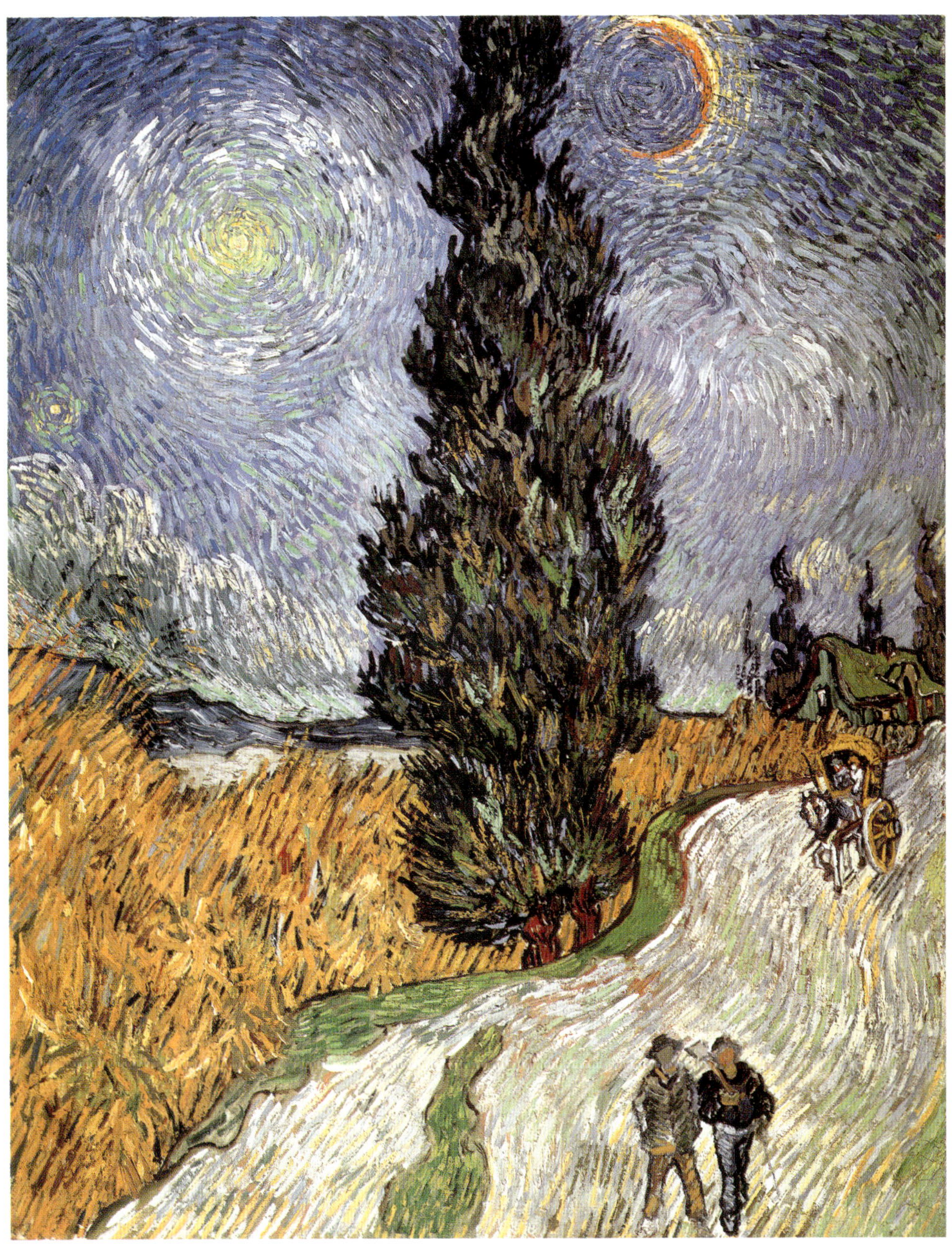

Sources of Quotations

Introduction, page 6
'You know the landscape there, superb trees full of majesty and serenity…'
Letter 381, to Theo van Gogh, on or about 5 September 1883

Chapter 1, page 15
'And in all of nature, in trees for instance, I see expression and a soul, as it were.'
Letter 292, to Theo van Gogh, Sunday 10 December 1882

Chapter 2, page 35
'Imagine, right then, an avenue of tall poplars with the autumn leaves…'
Letter 402, to Theo van Gogh, Friday 2 November 1883

Chapter 3, page 55
'And yet it's really beautiful in the city sometimes, don't you agree?'
Letter 361, to Theo van Gogh, on or about Wednesday 11 July, 1883

Chapter 4, page 73
'This rage to paint orchards won't last forever.'
Letter 594, to Theo van Gogh, Monday 9 April 1888

Chapter 5, page 95
'Now, better than in the beginning, I see the real countryside of Provence…'
Letter 841, to Wil van Gogh, Monday 20 January 1890

Further Reading

Van Gogh's Correspondence
Vincent van Gogh, *Vincent van Gogh – The Letters*, 6 vols (London & New York: Thames & Hudson, 2009)
Vincent van Gogh, *The Real Van Gogh: The Artist and His Letters* (London: Royal Academy of Arts, 2010)

Van Gogh's Drawings
Ives, Colta F., Susan A. Stein, Sjraar van Heugten and Marije Vellekoop, *Vincent van Gogh: The Drawings* (New York: Metropolitan Museum of Art; Amsterdam: Van Gogh Museum; New Haven: Yale University Press, 2005)
Van Heugten, Sjraar, and Roelie Zwikker, *Vincent van Gogh: Drawings*, 4 vols (Amsterdam: Van Gogh Museum; Aldershot, UK: Lund Humphries, 1996–2007)
Van Heugten, Sjraar, Marije Vellekoop and Roelie Zwikker, *Van Gogh: The Master Draughtsman* (London: Thames & Hudson, 2005)

Van Gogh's Paintings
Bailey, Martin, *Van Gogh and Britain: Pioneer Collectors* (Edinburgh: National Galleries of Scotland, 2006)
Thomson, Belinda, *Van Gogh Paintings: The Masterpieces* (London: Thames & Hudson, 2007)
Walther, Ingo F., and Rainer Metzger, *Van Gogh: The Complete Paintings* (Cologne: Taschen, 1997)

Van Gogh and Romanticism
Rosenblum, Robert, *Modern Painting and the Northern Romantic Tradition: Friedrich to Rothko* (London: Thames & Hudson, 1975)

Van Gogh and Gauguin

Druick, Douglas W., and Peter Kort Zegers, *Van Gogh and Gauguin: The Studio of the South*
    (London: Thames & Hudson, 2001)

Gayford, Martin, *The Yellow House: Van Gogh, Gauguin and Nine Turbulent Weeks in Arles*
    (London: Fig Tree/Penguin Books, 2006)

Psychological Factors

Lubin, Albert J., *Stranger on the Earth: A Psychological Biography of Vincent van Gogh* (New York:
    Da Capo Press, 1996)

Jamison, Kay Redfield, *Touched with Fire: Manic-Depressive Illness and the Artistic Temperament*
    (New York: Free Press/Simon & Schuster, 1994)

Biographical Context

Naifeh, Steven, and Gregory White Smith, *Van Gogh: The Life* (London: Profile Books, 2011)

Picture Credits

All works are by Vincent van Gogh, unless otherwise stated. They are listed by their full titles, and measurements are given, where known, in centimetres (and inches), height before width. Bracketed numerals indicate the image number. The list is ordered alphabetically according to the cities where the holding institutions are located.

Amsterdam, Van Gogh Museum, (Vincent van Gogh Foundation): [3] Sketch in Letter 542 (to Theo van Gogh), 13.1 x 17.3 (5 ⅛ x 6 ¾). [5] *Rocks and Trees*, 49.1 x 61 (19 x 24). [6] *Canal*, 25.4 x 25.8 (10 x 10 ⅛). [8] *The Kingfisher*, 40.2 x 54.2 (15 ⅞ x 21 ⅜). [9] *Tree Roots and Trunks*, 69.8 x 119.7 (27 ½ x 47 ⅛). [11] *Landscape in Stormy Weather*, 29.7 x 22.6 (11 ¾ x 8 ⅞). [12] *Landscape at Twilight*, 70 x 121 (27 ½ x 47 ⅝). [16] *Small Pear Tree in Blossom*, 91.5 x 64 (36 x 25). [17] *The Sower*, 32.5 x 40.3 (12 ¾ x 15 ⅞). [25] *Pine Trees in the Fen*, 35.8 x 45 (14 ⅛ x 17 ¾). [26] *Pollard Birches*, 39.5 x 54.2 (15 ½ x 21 ⅜). [29] *Winter Garden*, 40.3 x 54.6 (15 ⅞ x 21 ½). [32] *Avenue of Poplars*, 54.2 x 39.3 (21 ⅜ x 15 ½). [38] *A Guinguette*, 38.7 x 52.5 (15 ¼ x 20 ⅝). [39] *The Entrance to the Moulin de la Galette*, 31.6 x 24 (12 ½ x 9 ½). [54] *The White Orchard or Provençal Orchard*, 39.5 x 53.6 (15 ½ x 21 ⅛). [57] *Branches with Almond Blossom*, 73.3 x 92.4 (28 ⅞ x 36 ⅜). [71] *Road with Pine Trees*, 24.8 x 32.4 (9 ¾ x 12 ¾). **Baltimore Museum of Art, Cone Collection**: [70] *Landscape with Trees and Figures*, 49.9 x 65.4 (19 ⅝ x 25 ¾). **Cambridge, Fitzwilliam Museum**: [7] *Autumn Landscape*, 66.9 x 88.3 (26 ⅜ x 34 ¾). [13] *Couple Walking between Rows of Poplars*, 50 x 100.5 (19 ⅝ x 39 ⅝). **Cleveland Museum of Art**: [2] *The Poplars at Saint-Rémy*, 61.6 x 45.7 (24 ¼ x 18). **Edinburgh, National Gallery of Scotland**: [49] *Orchard in Blossom, (Apricot Trees)*, 55 x 65 (21 ⅝ x 25 ⅝). **Göteborgs Konstmuseum**: [62] *Olive Grove*, 74 x 93 (29 ⅛ x 36 ⅝). **Houston, Menil Collection**: [45] *A Corner of a Garden in the Place Lamartine*, 24.1 x 31.5 (9 ½ x 12 ⅜). **Houston, Museum of Fine Arts**: [66] *Rocks with Oak Tree*, 54 x 65 (21 ¼ x 25 ⅝). **Kiel, Pommern Foundation**: [64] *A Lane Near Arles*, 61 x 50 (24 x 19 ⅝). **London, British Museum**: [28] Rembrandt van Rijn, *The Three Trees*, 21.3 x 27.9 (8 ⅜ x 11). **London, Courtauld Gallery, Samuel Courtauld Trust**: [56] *Peach Blossom in the Crau*, 65.5 x 81.5 (25 ¾ x 32 ⅛). **London, National Gallery**: [74] *A Wheatfield with Cypresses*, 72.5 x 91.5 (28 ½ x 36). **Los Angeles, Armand Hammer Museum of Art and Cultural Center**: [30] *The Parsonage Garden at Nuenen in the Snow*, 53 x 78 (20 ⅞ x 30 ¾). **Madrid, Museo Thyssen-Bornemisza**: [19] *Landscape at Dusk*, 35 x 43 (13 ¾ x 16 ⅞). Photo Scala, Florence. **Minneapolis Institute of Arts**: [61] *Olive Trees with Yellow Sky and Sun*, 73.7 x 92.7 (29 x 36 ½). **New York, Brooklyn Museum**: [73] *Cypresses*, 62.2 x 47.1 (24 ½ x 18 ½). **New York, Collection Joseph H. Hazen**: [4] *The Grove*, 73 x 92

(28 ¾ x 36 ½). **New York, Glen Falls, Hyde Collection**: [52] *Orchard with Arles in the Background*, 53.2 x 38.8 (21 x 15 ¼).
New York, Metropolitan Museum of Art: [1] *Road in Etten*, 39.4 x 57.8 (15 ½ x 22 ¾), Robert Lehman Collection,
1975 (1975.1.774). [53] *Flowering Orchard*, 72.4 x 53.3 (28 ½ x 21), The Mr. and Mrs. Henry Ittleson Jr. Purchase Fund, 1956
(56.13). [63] *Olive Picking*, 72.7 x 91.4 (28 ⅝ x 36), The Walter H. and Leonore Annenberg Collection, Gift of Walter H.
and Leonore Annenberg, 1995, Bequest of Walter H. Annenberg, 2002 (1995.535). [72] *Cypresses*, 93.4 x 74 (36 ¾ x 29 ⅛),
Rogers Fund, 1949 (49.30). **New York, Museum of Modern Art**: [60] *Olive Trees with the Alpilles in the Background*,
72.5 x 92 (28 ¼ x 36 ½), Mrs John Hay Whitney Bequest, 1998 (581.1998). **New York, Solomon R. Guggenheim Museum**,
Thannhauser Collection: [65] *The Road to Tarascon*, 23.2 x 31.9 (9 ⅛ x 12 ½). **Oslo, Nasjonalmuseet/Nasjonalgalleriet**:
[67] *View of Arles from Montmajour*, 48.6 x 60 (19 ⅛ x 23 ⅝). **Otterlo, Netherlands, Kröller-Müller Museum**: [14] *Study
of a Tree*, 50 x 69 (19 ⅝ x 27 ⅛). [20] *Edge of a Wood*, 34.5 x 49 (13 ⅛ x 19 ½). [22] *Girl in a Wood*, 39 x 59 (15 ⅜ x 23 ½). [27] *Autumn
Landscape with Four Trees*, 64 x 89 (25 ½ x 35). [31] *Avenue of Poplars at Sunset*, 45.5 x 32.5 (17 ⅞ x 12 ¾). [36] *The Paddemoes*,
25 x 31 (9 ⅞ x 12 ¼). [43] *Les Alyscamps, Falling Autumn Leaves*, 73 x 92 (28 ¾ x 36 ½). [50] *Orchard Bordered by Cypresses*, 65 x 81
(25 ⅝ x 37 ⅞). [55] *Peach Tree in Blossom, 'Souvenir de Mauve'*, 73 x 59.5 (28 ¾ x 23 ⅜). [58] *Olive Grove*, 72 x 92 (28 ⅜ x 36 ¼).
[68] *Willows at Sunset*, 31.5 x 34.5 (12 ⅜ x 13≈⅝). [75] *Road with Cypress and Star*, 92 x 73 (36 ¼ x 28 ¾). **Paris, Musée Rodin**:
[37] *Avenue of Plane Trees near Arles Station*, 46 x 49.5 (18 ⅛ x 19 ½). **Pasadena, Norton Simon Art Foundation**: [10] *The
Mulberry Tree*, 54 x 65 (21 ¼ x 25 ⅝). Photo Bridgeman Art Library. **Private Collection**: [23] *Pollard Willow*, 38 x 56 (15 x 22).
[24] *Landscape in Drenthe*, 27.5 x 42 (10 ⅞ x 16 ½). [33] *Country Lane with Two Figures*, 32 x 39.5 (12 ⅝ x 15 ½). Photo Christie's
Images Ltd./SuperStock. [35] *Les Alyscamps*, 93 x 72 (36 ⅝ x 28 ⅜). [41] *Scene in a Park*, 46.5 x 37 (18 ¼ x 14 ⅝). [42] *On the
Outskirts of Paris*, 38 x 46 (15 x 18 ⅛). [44] *Avenue with Flowering Chestnut Trees*, 72.5 x 92 (28 ½ x 36 ¼). [46] *Chestnut Trees in
Blossom*, 70 x 58 (27 ½ x 22 ⅞). Photo Bridgeman Art Library. [48] *Orchard with Pear Trees in Blossom*, 72 x 59 (28 ⅜ x 23 ¼).
[51] *Orchard with Peach Blossom*, 65 x 81 (25 ⅝ x 31 ⅞). [69] *The Old Yew*, 91 x 71 (35 ⅞ x 28). **Rotterdam, Museum Boijmans
Van Beuningen**: [18] *Avenue of Poplars*, 78 x 98 (30 ¾ x 38 ⅝). [21] *Orchard*. **Shawnee Mission, Kansas, Collection
Henry W. Block**: [34] *The Rispal Restaurant at Asnières*, 72 x 60 (28 ⅜ x 23 ⅝). **Musée des Beaux Arts de Tournai**: [59]
Olive Trees: Montmajour, 48 x 60 (18 ⅞ x 23 ⅝). **Walsall Museum and Art Gallery**: [15] *Sorrow*, 44.5 x 27 (17 ½ x 10 ⅝).
Washington, D.C., Phillips Collection: [40] *The Road Menders*, 71 x 93 (28 x 36 ⅝). **Zurich, Foundation E. G. Bührle
Collection**: [47] *Blossoming Chestnut Branches*, 72 x 91 (28 ⅜ x 35 ⅞).